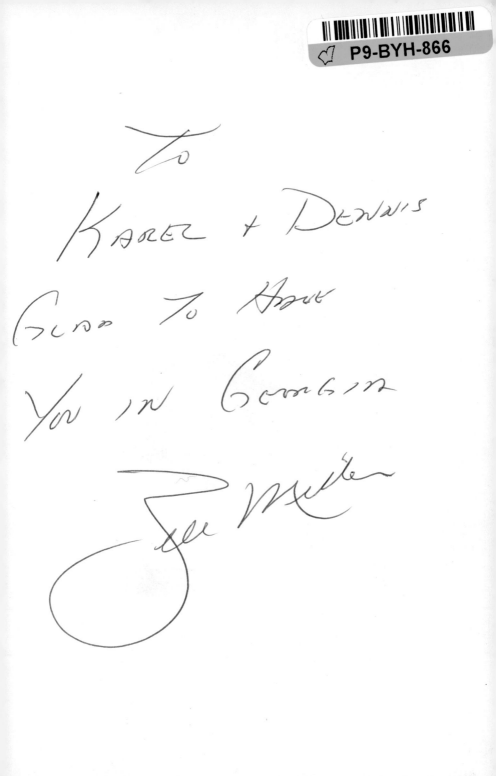

To

Karel + Dennis

Good To Have

You in Georgia

Zell Miller

THEY HEARD GEORGIA SINGING

Great Georgians—Volume 2

By
Zell Miller

**Published by
ADVOCATE PRESS
Franklin Springs, Georgia**

Also by Zell Miller

THE MOUNTAINS WITHIN ME (1976)

GREAT GEORGIANS (1983)

DEDICATION

**In Memory
of
MARY TALLENT**

CONTENTS

CONTENTS

CONTENTS

ACKNOWLEDGEMENTS

Of the many people who have contributed substantially in my behalf, I would like to thank the staff of the Country Music Foundation for assistance and guidance in their archives.

In addition, my sincere thanks goes to Cotton Carrier, Bill Lowery, Don Rhodes, Lee Roy Abernathy and the others who shared their warehouse of knowledge with me.

To Edna Herren, who has been correcting and reviewing my manuscripts since I was her student at Young Harris College, I again express thanks.

I especially thank those who coaxed me through troubled times when the enormity of the task seemed overwhelming. They know who they are.

To my wife, Shirley, who encourages me to write and do research even though I do it in weird spurts and pile the material all over everywhere, thank you again.

As with the many other things I do, I must thank my staff without whose great ability to do the day-by-day chores I would not have time for such pursuits (Martha Gilland, Marti Pingree, Sarah Eby-Ebersole, Mary Beazley, Amelia Key, Elizabeth Martin, Donna Blankinship, "Cap" Hicks and John Slaton). and especially Bill Burson for taking the time at night to read, criticize and offer excellent advice.

And for the inspiration, I thank all the songwriters and artists who have touched my life over the years.

INTRODUCTION

The selection of the City of Atlanta by the National Academy of Recording Arts and Sciences (NARAS) over Memphis, Los Angeles and other recording centers of the nation as the site for its Grammy Hall of Fame gave official recognition to the facts that the State of Georgia not only is the home of many of the foremost performing artists of the present and past but also has developed into one of the leading areas in the music industry of the United States.

Georgia is not a johnny-come lately to musical leadership. While Tin Pan Alley, Hollywood and Vine and Beale Street may have had more publicity and may have been more commercial over the years, Georgia has been in the forefront of musical pioneering. Atlanta's radio station WSB put Fiddlin' John Carson on the air in 1922 and Okeh Records set up a studio in Atlanta to record his "hillbilly" tunes the following year. The Voice of the South under the directional genius of "The Little Colonel," Lambdin Kay, set national trends throughout the early days of broadcasting in encouraging musicians to present themselves on the airwaves and built upon that foundation under the far-sighted leadership of J. Leonard Reinsch, who made the WSB Barn Dance and stars like Hank Penny, James and Martha Carson and the Swanee River Boys the models for the programs and performers that would emulate them on other radio, and later television, stations throughout the nation.

Georgia Tech's Radio Station, WGST, put Georgia on the road to becoming a recording center by allowing its studios to be used by Bill Lowery to make some of his first hit recordings, including Ray Charles' first big hit, and set the stage for the development of his music recording and publishing conglomerate, The Lowery Group, and its fabulous string of superstars like Ray Stevens, Jerry Reed, Brenda Lee, Joe South, the Tams, Alicia Bridges and many others whose careers will be treated in this book.

Zenas "Daddy" Sears, the white owner of Atlanta's major black radio station, WAOK, has been one of the nation's foremost developers and producers of black rhythm and blues artists, and Phil Walden, of Macon's Capricorn Records, was the national leader in the development of rock bands like the Allman

Brothers, Marshall Tucker and Dixie Dregs. Buddy Buie built one of the nation's most modern and efficient recording enterprises in his acclaimed Studio One operation in Doraville, Georgia, and was the guiding genius behind the development of the Classics IV, Lynard Skynard and the Atlanta Rhythm Section, the superband which, with the promotional assistance of Alex Cooley (whose Southeast Music Hall became the gathering place of the nation's foremost musical groups) filled Georgia Tech's Grant Stadium twice for "Champagne Jam" concerts.

Artists from throughout the world now come to Lowery and Buie for professional advance and production assistance, and one of the fastest-rising recording labels in the nation is Atlanta's new Katz Family Records established by Entertainment Attorney Joel Katz.

Perhaps the greatest strength of Georgia's Music Industry is its diversity, covering the spectrum of black artists from Gospel Singer Thomas Dorsey and Soul Singer James Brown to Opera Singer Jessye Norman and of white artists from Country Singer Bill Anderson and Gospel Singer Hovie Lister to Folk Singer Hedy West and Symphony and Choral Conductor Robert Shaw.

Its concerts run the gamut from those of the Atlanta Symphony Orchestra in Chastain Park, to which thousands bring gourmet picnic baskets and candelabra to wine and dine, to a mix of popular and classical music each week during the summer to those by gospel groups at the Joyful Noise Christian Night Club in East Point, where the strongest beverage served is coffee. There are also the highly-successful music parks operated throughout the State attracting sell-out crowds to hear top country artists. The Swampland Opera at Toomsboro, weekly attracts hundreds to dine on home-cooked meals while listening to performances of local artists and groups trying to make their places in the worlds of country and gospel music. Pioneered by "Mama" Wynette Mitchem, country music nightclubs have flourished in the Atlanta Area. All-night Gospel Sings are popular and followers of the ancient system of singing by shaped notes hold an annual Sacred Harp Sing, using the hymnal first compiled in 1844 by Georgians Franklin White and E. L. King.

Because there exists no ready reference work on the many

10

personalities who have brought Georgia to musical greatness, I have endeavored with this volume to compile brief musical biographies of those men and women who have made major contributions to Georgia Musical History either as native sons and daughters or as major personalities within the context of Georgia Music.

The criterion for selection for inclusion has been narrower than that of merely being born in, passing through or coming into the state after achieving fame and making contributions elsewhere. The application of that yardstick excluded, for example, Bandleader Harry James, who was born in Albany, Georgia, simply because the Mighty Haig Circus with whom his parents performed happened to be there at the time; Singer Lena Horne, who lived with relatives and attended school in the fifth, sixth and seventh grades in Fort Valley and Atlanta; Grammy Winner — Gospel Singer Amy Grant, who was born in Augusta; and Country Music Superstar Kenny Rogers, who recently built a home and established a cattle and horse ranch in Oglethorpe County after marrying Hee Haw Personality Marianne Gordon of Athens.

In doing my research for this book, I discovered many little known facts about Georgia contributions to music which I have tried to include, like that the song "Luckenbach, Texas," which is the theme song of the country music outlaws of the Willie Nelson-Waylon Jennings School, was written by Georgian Chips Moman, who now is a music producer in Nashville, Tennessee.

I have endeavored to put them together in a manner which will be both informative and enjoyable to read and will serve to give readers a full perspective of how Georgia music of today represents a blending of the black rhythm and blues music of the fields of South Georgia and the white traditional folk music of the mountains of North Georgia into the urban sounds of the metropolitan recording studios of Atlanta and Macon that are rapidly being homogenized into a common music embracing classical, country, gospel, rock, soul and rhythm and blues which is enjoyed, appreciated and sung by people of all ages and classes regardless of color, economic status or place of residence.

— ZELL MILLER

11

LEE ROY ABERNATHY

The term "living legend" was coined for Lee Roy Abernathy, the colorful singer, composer, professor, impresario, innovator and entrepreneur from Canton, Georgia, who is called "Gospel Music Patriarch" by The History of Gospel Music and whose Hall of Fame School of Music attracts drive-and-fly-in students from as far away as California. Lee Roy has been larger than life in everything he has done during his 71 years from walking weekly to Atlanta to study conservatory music at the age of 15 to writing the first singing commercials and devising and offering the world's only "guaranteed-to-play" piano course.

He can lay claim to writing campaign songs for both Franklin D. Roosevelt and Eugene Talmadge, composing one of the all-time-best-selling gospel songs, being the first publisher of gospel sheet music, inventing a typesetting system for setting music and membership in the Gospel Music Hall of Fame since 1973.

Abernathy can boast literally to being "born into gospel music." His father, Dee Abernathy, was a gospel songwriter and his mother, Clara, took him in her arms when the three of them went to singing school three weeks after his birth on Friday the 13th of August, 1913, in the little North Georgia textile village of Atco. He had to stand on a Coca-Cola crate to sing first tenor in The Atco Quartet at the age of five and was tenor for the quartet five years later when they cut their first record with Columbia.

Two years later his singing career was brought to an end for the next 20 years because of impacted tonsils which required extensive throat surgery, but he continued with the group as its piano player when his sister Velma quit that spot to get married. When he was 14, a better job for his father at Canton Cotton Mill took him to the town which was to be his home intermittently and finally thereafter and he joined his father as piano player for the Abernathy Quartet he founded to sing at funerals in the area and accompanied the group at the age of 15 when it recorded "I'm Redeemed" and "Don't Forget To Pray" for RCA Victor. That year he also started his own quartet, the Modern Mountaineers, which made 50 Bluebird Records for $50 each and played an extensive schedule of theater, church and banquet engagements.

That same year a crisis and turning point was reached in his life when he was invited to play piano for The Electrical Workers Quartet in Atlanta which sang both popular and gospel music and he quickly discovered to his embarrassment and dismay that he could not read the pop music. He went back home, closeted himself in a dark room for four days as a failure and emerged with a vow that he would master all kinds of music so "there will never be anyone to set a piece of music in front of me that I can't play." That was the beginning of the development of the force in his life that he calls "PMA" — Positive Mental Attitude — which he teaches to all of his students and defined it in one of his songs in these words: "You can help to change the world if you'll just change, change your attitude."

Abernathy enrolled in the Atlanta Conservatory, taking 30-minute lessons each Saturday for the next three years; and, lacking any other means of transportation, walked the 49 miles to and from Canton each week, often "trotting the last 10 to 15 miles to get home in time for the play of the Men's Bible Class on Sunday mornings." He paid $5 for each of his lessons by walking from house to house giving music lessons for 25-cents each, an experience which planted in his mind the seeds for his famous mail-order piano course which he began offering 14 years later. At the age of 19 he married Louise Ammons, the 16-year-old daughter of the mill supervisor who later would fire him for tardiness, and the first piece of furniture they bought for their cotton mill village house was a piano — purchased even before they owned a bed.

Taking unemployment with PMA and as a signal to get on with his music career, Abernathy opened Lee Roy's Music Store in Dalton where he taught private music lessons, organized and played in his own quartet and began writing his piano course. He and his father wrote songs together, including "Won't We Have A Good Time" and "My Labor Will Be O'er" and one of his father's solo efforts, "Don't Be Knockin' " was recorded by the Kingsmen. He began making movies of talent shows and gospel singings and was the first to use recording equipment and public address systems at gospel sings; wrote the 1936 campaign song for FDR, "Good Times Are Coming Soon," which had to be

14

shelved after the NRA was declared unconstitutional; wrote Gene Talmadge's famous "$3-Dollar Tag Song" and personally hawked copies at Talmadge rallies for a nickle each, often making as much as $100 a Saturday; recorded the Speer Family's first record in 1936; and conducted the first and only singing school ever taught on radio over Station WBLJ in Dalton.

In 1942 he was the first to introduce piano arrangements of the gospel music and in 1943 published the first sheet music in the gospel world, his own "I'll Thank My Savior For It." Despite ridicule from other gospel groups which sold their songs in books rather than individually, he proved he could sell more of his single copies for 50 cents than they could of their books for only 35 cents. That same year he and Louise moved to Chattanooga, Tennessee, where he organized the Four Tones with which he toured the country doing U. S. O. shows for servicemen. When two members of the quartet were drafted, the group was disbanded and Abernathy went to Atlanta where he joined Billy Carrier, George Hughes and Bill Lyles in reforming the Swanee River Boys, followed by a stint in Richmond, Virginia, playing the piano for the Rangers Quartet featured on Station WRVA. In 1945 he completed his mail-order piano course after eight years of work which, although the subject of many jokes, proved exceedingly popular and profitable and subsequently has been offered throughout the world in every country having dependable post offices available to the general public.

It was during this period that he narrowly missed being a victim of Atlanta's tragic Winecoff Hotel fire, about which he wrote the controversial song, "The Burning Of The Winecoff," which received the National Fire Protection Award in 1946. Although Abernathy had a permanent room at the hotel and usually stayed there because of the gasoline shortage, he had been able to go home on the weekend of the fire because a friend had given him a coupon for three gallons of gas.

In 1946 Lee Roy introduced the "Battle of Songs" in Atlanta between himself and the Rangers and Hovie Lister and the Homeland Harmony Quartet. Later that year he joined the Homeland Harmony group which subsequently recorded his hit song, "Everybody's Gonna Have A Wonderful Time Up There," which swept the country under the title of "Gospel Boogie," selling more than five million records and covered by almost every gospel group in the nation as well as by such popular and country singers as Pat Boone, Johnny Mathis and Johnny Cash. He and the group were the subject of much national publicity, including major articles in Billboard and Radio Mirror. In 1947 he and Homeland Harmony appeared on a closed circuit television show in Atlanta for which he quickly wrote a special song entitled "Television" after being asked by the producer to do "something different." That also was the year he wrote his book, "it," which now is out of print but is a classic account of historical gospel events.

Lee Roy and Shorty Bradford with whom he had worked off and on since 1939 left Homeland Harmony in 1949 to form the Happy Two and make cross-country tours for television shows, recordings, backup work and commercials. It was during this time that Lee Roy wrote the nation's first singing commercials — the most famous of which was "You'd Better Get Wild Root Cream Oil, Charlie." Other memorable ones were for Halo Shampoo and B-Brand Insect Spray. The popularity of the Happy Two brought them an invitiation to do a daily television show on WAGA-TV in Atlanta beginning in 1951 and it continued five nights weekly for seven years. At the height of its popularity it was rated No. 3 in the nation by both Neilson and Cash Box and virtually every gospel group in the country appeared as guests on the program during its course. Also during this time he formed several other quartets, including the Miracle Men and the Lee Roy Abernathy Quartet, and he and Bradford traveled more than 5 million miles for concerts and personal appearances throughout the United States and abroad.

In 1958 with a campaign chest of only $500, Lee Roy became a candidate for Governor of Georgia, traveling the byways of the State in a 40-foot road train with a red piano and a Coca-Cola crate for a bench. His campaign song was "Lee Roy's The Boy" sung to the tune of "Casey Jones." He didn't win the race but he attracted a lot of attention and much media coverage.

From 1959 until 1961 he studied for his doctorate in music at Golden Temple, Inc., in Knoxville and pursued other graduate studies in Chicago and Cincinnati. He also invented a typesetting system for setting music and in 1973 was elected to the Gospel Music Hall of Fame.

A pinched nerve forced him into temporary retirement for three years in 1969, but he now is fully recovered and spending most of his time giving voice lessons 50 to 60 times a week to students who come from throughout the Southeast and as far away as Texas and California. He has constructed a new, modern building complete with the most modern musical, sound and recording equipment for his Hall of Fame School of Music located across from his house in Canton. The bottom floor has a large stage and auditorium where he gives group singing lessons and does concerts. The upstairs is devoted to a museum featuring memorabilia of his long and colorful career and artifacts of the history of gospel music.

He has no plans to slow down but gives no thought to the future. Says he:

"I don't ever worry about the future because I've already lived four or five lifetimes."

Lee Roy Abernathy

The Allman Brothers Band

THE ALLMAN BROTHERS BAND

Duane and Gregg Allman and the other master musicians who were their compatriots in the Allman Brothers Band struggled for years for the success they finally achieved. In doing so they developed the "Macon, Georgia, Sound" which made their organization America's best answer to the British super groups which had dominated rock music prior to their emergence in the Seventies.

That the Allman Brothers Band was more than the "southern-fried boogie band," which some of its critics called it, is evidenced by the facts that it was integrated and that even after the tragic deaths of its two most talented members, Duane and Berry Oakley, it participated in July 1973 at Watkins Glen in the largest rock concert in history in which they costarred with the Grateful Dead.

In retrospect, the Allman Brothers Band must be credited with bringing rock music back to its no-frills roots of southern country, soul, rhythm and blues and jazz basics and establishing the soaring interplay and meticulous counterpoint of two lead guitars as the bedrock of America's new contemporary pop rock music. The group in its varying compositions both helped make and destroy Capricorn Records of Macon, Georgia, as the world's largest independent recording company. And, although there have been many imitators of his work and style, no one has come close to equalling Duane as a virtuoso slide guitarist. It is impossible to speculate what the band might have accomplished had it been able to maintain the creative momentum Duane inspired.

Howard Duane and Gregory Lenoir Allman were born within thirteen months of each other in Nashville, Tennessee. After the death of their soldier father by a hitchhiker they moved with their mother in 1959 to Daytona Beach, Florida, where she became a CPA. Much to her dismay, they became contemporaries of black blues musicians. Duane first wrecked a motorcycle and then dropped out of school to teach himself to play the guitar as Gregg already did. They soon had their own school dance band, the Y-Teens, and in 1963 joined an integrated rock group called the House Rockers.

When Gregg graduated from high school in 1965 they went to St. Louis where they organized a band called the Allman Joys and enjoyed fair success playing honky-tonks and go-go bars. They did two albums, including a psychedelic single of the Willie Dixon blues number, "Spoonful," which were released on Did Records.

When the band folded in 1967, they went to Los Angeles at the suggestion of Bill McKuen, manager of the Nitty Gritty Dirt Band and joined three Alabama musicians to form Hourglass. They signed a recording contract with Liberty Records which produced two bland, unsuccessful albums and threatened them with prosecution when they headed back home after becoming discouraged and fed up with living in "garbage motels."

In 1968 they teamed up briefly with drummer Butch Trucks band, the "31st of February," before Duane was invited by Rick Hall of Fame Studios to come to Muscle Shoals to back Wilson Pickett and convinced him to do his hit cover of the Beatles' "Hey, Jude." Intimidated by Liberty Records, Gregg returned to California to complete their contract. Hall signed Duane to a contract which he sold to Jerry Wexler, of Atlantic Records, who sold it to Phil Walden of Macon, Otis Redding's former manager, as part of a deal in which Walden was to set up Capricorn as a custom label to be distributed by Atlantic.

Walden called Duane and asked him to assemble a band; and, taking Jaimoe (Jai Johnny) Johanson, with whom he had played in Alabama, Duane went to Jacksonville where they slept on the floor at Truck's place and jammed with them and two members of a band known as "Second Coming," lead guitarist Dickey Betts and bassist Berry Oakley, after which he stood in the doorway and declared: "Anybody in this room that's not gonna play in my band, you're gonna have to fight your way out."

It was March 1969 when he sent a telegram to Gregg to come back to be organist and vocalist and Gregg later recalled it arrived just as he was "building up nerve to put a pistol to my head." They moved to Macon where they lived in two rooms with a bath that did not work and slept on the floor on five double mattresses. They recorded their first Capricorn album, "The

Allman Brothers Band," in New York that summer. It won critical acclaim but enjoyed little success and they hit the road to do 500 concerts in the next two years. Their resources were so meager that they traveled in an Econoline van with eleven of them sleeping on two mattresses. At one time they were so broke they had to panhandle enough money to pay the toll across the Golden Gate Bridge to do a gig in Fillmore West.

If it had not been for Duane returning periodically to Muscle Shoals for session work, they might not have made it at all. It was in Alabama that Duane began building his reputation as a top guitarist by backing such stars as Aretha Franklin and doing the slide work on Eric Clapton's "Layla" by Derek and the Dominoes.

They did their second album, "Idlewild South" in October 1969, but it too, was disappointing. Deciding they could not capture the awesome power of their concert performances in a studio, they achieved their breakthrough by doing their third album live. It was a double disc done in New York and titled "At the Fillmore East" and it became the band's first gold record when released in 1971. It contained only seven songs but among them were the band's classic versions of "Statesboro Blues," "Hot Lanta," "Stormy Monday," "You Don't Love Me," "In Memory of Elizabeth Reed" and "Whipping Post."

With the thunderous bass of Oakley, the climbing call-and-response guitar duets and mercurial solos of Duane and Dickey and Gregg's growling vocals and inventive organ, it captured the Allmans at their artistic peak and caused their popularity to soar like wildfire and their income to pyramid accordingly.

It was when they took their first vacation to enjoy the fruits of their labors that Duane was crushed to death in Macon on October 29, 1971, when his motorcycle skidded as he swerved to avoid an oncoming truck. His funeral was a media event in which the remaining band joined by other musicians from throughout the country staged a concert of his music behind the casket.

Oakley, who admired and sought to emulate Duane, never got over his depression and died in an almost identical motorcycle accident within three blocks of the first a little over a year later on November 11, 1972.

The band regrouped under Gregg and in late 1971 finished the album it had begun with Duane, "Eat A Peach," which went to platinum and yielded three chart singles, "Ain't Wasting Time No More," "Melissa" and "One Way Out." Chuck Leavell, a superb

21

musician who later toured with the Rolling Stones and at that time had played with the American Eagles and Sundown was recruited to replace Duane and bassist Lamar Williams from the Deep South Spiritual Singers was tapped to take Oakley's place.

Even without its two foremost talents, the group found its greatest popularity with its Watkins Glen performance in July 1973 and the August release of its smash fifth album, "Brothers and Sisters," which sold more than two million copies and brought a No. 1 single with Betts' "Ramblin' Man."

But the success was also accompanied by excessive indulgence. They bought their own private jet and a 34-member crew was hired to look after their every wish. Gregg's marriage to Cher Bono, the birth of their son, Elijah Blue, and the divorce were all media sensations as was a 1976 jury trial in Macon.

These things plus the continuing dispute over the band's direction between Leavell who wanted to go jazzier and Betts who insisted on more country in their sound resulted in the group's disintegration in late 1975.

Although several albums of their works were subsequently released, they did not get back together until 1979 when Gregg, Dickey, Butch and Jaimoe reconstituted the Band with the additions of guitarist Dan Tobler and bassist David Goldflies for an album and tour.

Gregg has since formed his own Gregg Allman Band and at the age of 35 in 1983 was attempting a comeback.

In 1982 Duane was inducted to the Georgia Music Hall of Fame with Gregg and his mother accepting the award.

BILL ANDERSON

Perhaps the truest measure of success of country music superstar Whispering Bill Anderson of Avondale Estates, Georgia, is that Billboard Magazine ranks him alongside his boyhood idol, Hank Williams, as one of the "True All-Time Greatest Contry Music Songwriters." And, if that is not enough, add that, with fifty, he holds more BMI Awards than any other composer and that he was elected to the Country Music Songwriters Hall of Fame before the age of forty.

The great irony of the career of James William Anderson II, is that while he did not grow up in poverty like many of his country music contemporaries, he probably is best known for his classic song about poverty, "Po' Folks," which gave the name to his band, one of the finest in the business, and the chain of restaurants with which his name is associated.

Born November 1, 1937, in Columbia, South Carolina, he was reared in Griffin and Decatur, Georgia, was torn to emulate Williams in music and Stan Musial in baseball and gave up the latter to humor his mother's wish that he go to college. While studying journalism at The University of Georgia, he first covered sports for a Decatur weekly and the Atlanta dailies and then became a disc jockey, commuting from Athens to nearby Commerce where he performed on an afternoon show with a rubber duck called "Josh" and started writing and recording songs which he tried to sell through the mail order house of TNT Records of San Antonio, Texas.

One of the songs was "City Lights," which he penned while sitting one night on the roof of the tallest building in Commerce, the three-story Andrew Jackson Hotel, and which TNT dismissed by pressing only 500 copies and sending them to Anderson for personal distribution. He sent copies to fellow deejays and when Ray Price caught it on his car radio, he pronounced it "the best song I ever heard" and scrapped a recording he had scheduled for the following week in favor of it.

Bill Anderson

"City Lights" became the Number One Song of 1955, earned a Gold Record and became an all-time country hit that decided Anderson on a musical career which he launched disastrously with a road trip with Roger Miller that ended with their car breaking down in Arizona and their having to hock their record player to get back home. But, after finishing work on his degree in 1959, he headed to Nashville where that year another of his compositions, "That's What It's Like To Be Lonesome," made the Top Ten and he signed a contract with Decca (now MCA) Records.

In 1960 he made top-chart levels with "Tips of My Fingers" which he recorded himself. The next year he wrote "Happy Birthday to Me," for Hank Locklin and did "Walk Out Backward" and the smash "Po' Folks" for himself, followed by a crossover hit "Mama Sang A Song" in 1962. But it was in 1963 that he had his greatest year with "Still" which made it to the top in both the country and pop charts, brought him a Gold Record, was named Variety Magazine's No. 1 Song of the Year and won him recognition as both Male Vocalist and Top Country Songwriter of the Year, titles he would subsequently repeat four times in both categories. He had a second hit that year in "8 by 10" and scored his first international success when both were covered in England by Ken Dodd.

Most of his recordings of the Sixties were of his own songs among which were the hits, "I've Enjoyed As Much Of This As I Can Stand," "I Love You Drops," "I Get The Fever," "Wild Weekend," "My Life," and "But You Know I Love You." He took Alex Zanetis' "Me" to the top in 1964 and others of his works were recorded by Porter Wagoner, Faron Young, Charlie Louvin and Jean Shepherd.

He and Jan Howard won the first of his two Duet of the Year Awards with their "For Loving You" in 1967, the second coming in the next decade for his work with Mary Lou Turner, "That's What Makes Me Love You" and "Sometimes." In 1970 he had a change-of-pace hit with "Where Have All The Heroes Gone" and charted No. 2 with "Quits" and "The Corner of My Life."

In all he has more than 500 songs to his credit of which fifty-two have been single hits. He has done thrity-seven albums, received fifteen music trade paper awards and been a regular on the Grand Ole Opry since 1961.

Anderson was third only to Porter Wagoner and the Wilburn

Brothers in having a syndicated country music television show and his "The Bill Anderson Show" was seen for nine years in more than 100 cities coast-to-coast. He was the first country artist to host a network game show, doing ABC-TV's "The Better Sex," has appeared in the ABC soap opera "One Life To Live," is a frequent guest star on top variety, game and talk shows, is host of the nationally-syndicated television program "Backstage At The Grand Ole Opry" and is a featured star of the Nashville Cable Network. He has done five movies, composed and performed the title song for a sixth and narrated a seventh. He is an entrepreneur not only in the restaurant but also the music publishing business. His touring show logs 100,000 miles and over a hundred days of performances throughout the country each year.

His classmate, Billy Dilworth, who also is one of the ranking country deejays of the nation, calls the personable and soft-spoken Anderson "country music with style and class." Anderson, who objects to being called a "button-down hillbilly," denies being "goody-goody" and maintains that what he does is "just simply country music." He has avoided songs with certain overtones, having gone so far as to get Cal Smith to record his hit song, "The Lord Knows I'm Drinking;" Conway Twitty "I've Never Been to Heaven," Porter Wagoner "Cold Hard Facts of Life" and he is amused at the reactions of his breathy singing style which flocks of admiring women find sexy.

He attributes the success of his songs to "empathy" which he defines as "the ability to identify with other people — put yourself in another man's place, feel what he feels, think what he thinks."

He presently records for Southern Tracks, an Atlanta label.

26

WENDY BAGWELL
AND
THE SUNLITERS

Wendy Bagwell is an ex-Marine with a flair for telling funny stories and writing and arranging captivating music who, with his group the Sunliters, has made gospel singing fun the world over and collected a string of impressive awards to prove it.

Wendy, a successful businessman whose home is Smyrna, Georgia, has tickled the funny bones of people all around the globe with his hilarious accounts of his childhood escapades and the experiences of the other Sunliters and himself in their international travels. His recording, "Here Come the Rattlesnakes," not only became a gold record but also earned him a special award from the Gospel Music Association and selection as Comedian of the Year by Record World. He attributes the success of his comedy to the fact that, while other entertainers have experiences similar to those he relates, "They just have more sense than to get on stage and tell about them."

Jerri Morrison and Jan Buckner, the two female Sunliters, have been acclaimed for their unique blending harmony and "Little Jan," as she is called by the group, has received the Female Vocalist of the Year Award of the Gospel Music Association. She plays the piano, harp, bass guitar and other instruments and works with Wendy in writing and arranging all of the group's music. Jerri is a one-woman rhythm section with her tambourine, casabel and other percussion instruments and is called "Leather Lungs" by Wendy who credits her powerful voice for what he calls the fact that "hardly nobody knows I can't sing." The five men who complete the band play seven different instruments among themselves.

Attesting to the group's popularity abroad is its choice by the U. S. State Department to sponsor it on an extended tour of Europe and the presentation to it of the Showmanship Award of the United States Government. In addition to the numerous awards the Sunliters have received from the Academy of Recording Arts and Sciences, they also hold the Pioneer Award of the Southern Gospel Music Association and the Marvin Norcross Award presented by Singing News and considered the highest honor that can be bestowed on any person or group in the gospel music industry.

Wendy Bagwell and the Sunliters

RAZZY BAILEY

No country music star ever hit bottom harder or bounced to the top more spectacularly than Razzy Bailey, the poor kid who grew up in Big Snapper Creek in Alabama. He paid his dues in the honky-tonks of Georgia and Florida and now retires to the farm he bought near LaGrange to reflect upon the events of a checkered life which proves that truth is both stranger and more colorful than fiction.

Born on Valentine's Day in 1939 and named for his father, Erastus, a cotton mill laborer, sometime truck driver and amateur picker and songwriter, Razzy grew up without the comforts of indoor plumbing and electricity. He learned to play the guitar on an instrument "with a neck so warped it looked more like a bow and arrow," and to sing the blues from the black field hands with whom he worked. He took a leadership role in the Future Farmers of America so that he could play in the LaFayette, Alabama, chapter's band which he helped win second place in state competition.

From the time he put all his savings at the age of ten into making a dime store recording, his undeviating goal was to make it as a writer, singer and recorder of songs. His first job after graduating from high school was with a band playing a club between Columbus and LaGrange, Georgia, which was shut down four months later when the highway was closed.

He married his high school sweetheart, Sandra Pressley, at the age of nineteen and took a succession of daytime jobs as butcher, soft-drink delivery truck driver and insurance and furniture salesman to support his growing family and to subsidize his nighttime playing in whatever locales he could find a slot, including an Atlanta strip joint. The closest he came to success was when he persuaded Atlanta music publisher Bill Lowery to have Joe South, Billy Joe Royal and Freddy Weller record "9,999,999 Tears" a song he wrote which would become a hit a decade later, only to have it flop.

29

The longest musical engagement he had during this period was a trio he formed and appropriately named Daily Bread which became the house band for a club in Naples, Florida, for six months. He did some recordings, mostly on minor labels, and came to the attention of Joe Mascolo (who later would remember him when he moved to RCA) when he cut "Stolen Moments," "Dancing On Brimstone," "I Hate Hate," and "Peanut Butter" for MGM, none of which went anywhere at the time.

He moved to Macon in 1976 where he signed a contract with Phil Walden's Capricorn Records. His drinking, he admits, had become excessive and his wife took their children and left him. The Razzy Bailey story could have ended right there had he not turned in desperation to psychic June Mahoney of Cassadaga, Florida, who inspired him to listen to his "inner guts." She advised him to seek his release from Walden and predicted one of his songs would become a hit if he would go back to Nashville and try pitching them again. Shortly thereafter, Mascolo recommended Bailey's material to Dickie Lee whose re-recordings of "9,999,999 Tears" and "Peanut Butter" made the first a Number One Hit and carried the second to top-chart levels.

That opened the long-closed doors and RCA started to issue some of his singles in 1978. "What Time Do You Have To Be Back In Heaven" charted in August and lasted to the end of the year. In 1979 he had successes with "Tonight She's Going to Love Me," "If Love Had a Face," and "I Ain't Got No Business Doing Business Today."

Between 1980 and 1983 he had eight straight Top Ten smashes and five Number One Singles: "Loving Up A Storm," "I Keep Coming Back," "Friends," "Midnight Hauler," and "She Left Love All Over Me." As his name and sound became known, his way with translating heartaches and everyday experiences into songs with which the working public could identify put him in a role of successes. His work won him awards as New Male Vocalist of the Year from the Academy of Country Music and Record World and Cash Box Magazines. He has appeared on Hee Haw, Austin City Limits, the Mike Douglas Show, and has raised the prospect of doing movies which is the next dimension he wishes to add to his career.

Many persons, hearing him for the first time, are surprised to learn that he is white, and even Charlie Pride has commented upon the remarkable way in which Razzy has captured the bluesy

30

sound, saying, "You can get away with singing like a black; I can't." Bailey says his singing style and musical sound were not developed consciously but rather are the products of an upbringing in which he was "influenced a lot by black farm workers" with whom he toiled as a lad in "the most euthenic context for rural blues in the country, the Alabama fields." The result is what the critics call "a rich, butterscotch sound" in which "a tremulous, almost rhythm and blues lushness sticks to his voice."

Perhaps his greatest pleasure and satisfaction comes from the fact that he and his 69 year-old father, from whom he learned his soulful licks on the guitar and banjo, have teamed up as co-authors on several records.

Razzy Bailey

NORMAN BLAKE

Few but the most ardent purists among the devotees of bluegrass, folk and traditional music will recognize the name of Norman Blake.

But almost any music lover will know to whose work you refer if you mention that of the dynamic and stunning lead guitarist on Bob Dylan's "Nashville Skyline Rag" and Joan Baez' "The Night They Drove Old Dixie Down."

Small wonder then that this talented artist who was born in Chattanooga, Tennessee, in 1938 and grew up in Rising Fawn and Trenton, Georgia, has been named by Guitar Player Magazine as the nation's fourth "Best Country Guitarist" behind Roy Clark, Merle Travis and Jerry Reed.

His virtuosity in acoustic music and his mastery of the old-time style not only on the guitar but also on the mandolin, dobro, fiddle and autoharp has made him in great demand both as a back-up musician and a solo performer.

His Rising Fawn String Ensemble composed of himself on those instruments, his wife Nancy on cello and single-row accordian and James Bryan with a fiddle mastered under the tutelage of Bill Monroe has turned out some of the most versatile and successful acoustic albums of the last twenty years.

Since dropping out of high shcool to play mandolin for The Dixie Drifters, he has made guest appearances on the Grand Ole Opry, cut an acclaimed bluegrass album entitled "12 Sheets of Bluegrass," played with John Hartford, Vasser Clements and Tut Taylor who has called him "one of the finest guitar pickers alive," and toured as a back up musician with June Carter. This led to a stint as a regular on the Johnny Cash Television Show. He was also featured with the Nitty Gritty Dirt Band on its monster album, "Will the Circle be Unbroken."

Blake particularly loves to play traditional Appalachian music and mourns the demise of bluegrass popularity. Although much of his work follows the style of Doc Watson, he does not conform to any category of traditional, bluegrass or progressive music but combines elements of all and uses a thumb and a finger pick to mix in bass runs and Carter Family-style leads on the guitar.

He is a guitar-pickers guitar picker, a back porch down-home singer who adds authenticity to country music. His personal musical preference is railroad songs such as his "Last Train From Poor Valley" which is a classic.

Norman Blake

HAMILTON FREDERICK BOHANNON

One of the most innovative and creative of contemporary American musicians is Hamilton Frederick Bohannon, the former music teacher from Newnan, Georgia, known professionally by just his last name.

For five years, he was the house conductor for Motown Records and led his 27-piece band, Bohannon and the Motown Sound, in backing the recordings of such stars as Diana Ross and the Supremes, Gladys Knight and the Pips, Martha Reeves and the Vandellas, The Spinners, The Four Tops, The Temptations, The Miracles, Marvin Gaye and Smokey Robinson.

A graduate of Atlanta's Clark College in music education, Bohannon left the classroom to perform in a Georgia band with guitarist Jimi Hendrix and came to the attention of Stevie Wonder, who made him his drummer from 1965 through 1967 and paved the way for him to become musical head of the Motown operation. In that capacity he established "The Beat" as his musical trademark and became identified by both his soulful manner of conserving with the band and the ever-present flower in his lapel.

He wrote, arranged, directed, produced, and published music for drums and played drums for all of the compositions on all of the nine Motown albums he recorded. He became the first artist since the Beatles to have two top records on the singles charts in the same week. His 1978 album, "Summertown Grove," is considered a classic combination of jazz and disco tunes. Such notables as Grammy-winning arranger Jerry Hey and Michael Henderson, Wah-Wah Watson and Ray Parker, Jr. were members of his band.

He severed his connection with Motown when it moved to the west coast; he then signed with Mercury Records to do five popular albums, including his biggest hit, "Let's Start the

Dance," in the Seventies. He founded his own Phase II Records, Ltd., and in 1983 joined Charles Fach, who left Mercury to establish Compleat Records, in a joint recording venture of their two companies to issue another Bohannon album and single under the title of "Make Your Body Move," which he wrote, arranged and directed in collaboration with Ray Parker, Jr.

Hamilton Fredrick Bohannon

BRICK

Three young black men who formed a rock group called Hellaphenalie while studying at Atlanta's Morris Brown College were the nucleus of the group of five incredibly talented, college-trained musicians who translated the positive feelings they had in common about their southern heritage into a hybrid musical style combining soul, disco and jazz they called "Dazz." This musical group which they named Brick became one of the most popular and successful acts in the funk-rock scene since 1975.

Lead guitarist Regi Hargis-Hickman, who was born in Austin, Texas, and came to Atlanta to live with his grandparents, Bishop and Mrs. E. L. Hickman; bass guitarist and spokesman Ray Ransom, who is the son of a high school principal in Waycross, Georgia, and who was president of the Morris Brown Marching Band; and keyboardist Donald Nevins, of Macon, Georgia, who later left to pursue his own musical goals in New York City, were the Morris Brown originals in what became the multi-talented quintet.

Their ranks were expanded to include brass and reed man Jimmy Brown of Savannah, Georgia, with whom Ransom also played in an Atlanta group called "Dawn's Early Light," and drummer Eddie Irons, the son of a professor father and attorney mother who moved to Atlanta from Tallahassee, Florida, Irons met Hargis-Hickman and Nevins after leaving nearby Morehouse College to follow a solo musical career. All excellent singers, aspiring writers and multiple-instrument performers, they practiced at Eddie's house after forming as a group. They adopted the name Brick after Regi's inspiration while watching Eddie's father put in a brick pond. They agreed with Regi that the term "had nothing but positive connotations . . . something solid, hard, durable."

According to Ransom, the group was unanimous in the determination to achieve a dynamic band sound which would be both artistic and funky, yet have depth and use, but not surrender

Brick

to "high-tech sounds." He said they set out to capture "a southern feel or mood . . . a bluesy, jazzy sort of thing" which would not go "against the grain of what Brick is: five guys who live in Georgia among the trees, birds and crickets." The result was a team effort which transformed them into a tight, exuberant group of eminent musicians specializing in soul-disco-funk material and featuring fluid and mellifluous vocals over commandingly funky rhythm tracks.

Brick issued its first single "Musicmatic" independently in late 1975, and it made Billboard's soul singles chart and brought the group a contract with Bang (later Bang/CBS) Records. Its first album, "Good High," issued the next year and dedicated to Atlanta as "The Next Great Music City," went to Gold as did the featured single, "Dazz," and brought the group's musically-coined style to national attention.

Their second album, "Brick," was released in 1977 and certified Platinum in March of 1978, the presentation being made by Georgia Governor George Busbee. It featured three hit singles, "Dusic," which became a Gold Record, "Ain't Gonna Hurt Nobody" and "We Don't Wanna Sit Down, We Wanna Get Down."

A third album, "Stoneheart," in 1979 was highlighted by the hit single "Raise Your Hands" and a cut entitled "Marching Band" in which the group was joined by eleven of the nation's foremost college band percussionists. In 1980, their "Waiting on You" album produced two single hits, "Push, Push," and "All the Way." In 1981, Motown's Ray Parker, Jr., produced the "Summer Heat" LP in Los Angeles with its "Sweat 'Til You Get Wet" hit single and the unique "Seaside Vibes," in which the group turned a Hargis-Hickman original tune into a demonstration of its sound virtuosity by duplicating the sounds of the beach, from the roller skaters to the waves crashing on the shore.

In 1982, their "After 5" album was recorded at Monarch Studios in Alpharetta, Georgia, was produced jointly by Brick and Phil Benton and featured female vocalists Donna McElroy and Donna DeWitt. It earlier had used Josie James in its ballad, "I Want You To Know," which was part of the "Summer Heat" collection.

In 1978 Brick was the star of the Atlanta Jazz Festival; Atlanta Journal critic Scott Cain said the 50,000 fans found their music "irresistible."

ALICIA BRIDGES

Singer and Songwriter Alicia Bridges says music has "been the moving force in my life for as long as I can remember" and it was her total dedication to it that caused her to say "the hell with" a career behind a computer terminal in Charlotte, North Carolina. She came to Atlanta where she came to the attention of Music publisher Bill Lowery and scored a smash hit with her first recording of one of her own songs, "I Love The Nightlife."

Alicia's single-minded pursuit of a musical career had its beginning at the age of 10 on a cotton farm near Lawndale, North Carolina, when she asked her father to teach her how to play his four-string guitar. When she won a talent contest sponsored by a Shelby, North Carolina, radio station two years later and was denied the prize of performing on a local radio show because of her age, she convinced the rival station, WADA, to put her on if she could sell enough advertising to sponsor her own program which she did. She dropped out of college where she was studying physical education to work in a bank and then in advertising for Sears; but, in her words: "One day I said the hell with it. I didn't want to end up behind some computer terminal. I wanted to sing." And she got a job singing first at a Holiday Inn and then at a strip joint in Charlotte before relocating to sing in clubs in Atlanta where she met her current writing partner, Susan Hutcheson.

Her work came to Lowery's attention and he signed her to a contract with his organization and carried her and Susan to Studio One in Doraville where they recorded their hit. Since that time Alicia has concentrated on her writing and a leadership role in the Georgia Music Festival staged yearly as part of Georgia Music Week sponsored by the Music Industry Committee of the Georgia Senate.

Although her original interest in music was aroused by the rock 'n' roll of Elvis Presley whose "Don't Leave Me Now" was the song with which she won her first talent contest, Alicia now considers herself a true rhythm and blues singer in the mode of Tina Turner, Aretha Franklin, Gladys Knight and Patti Labell.

She says listening to black singers like Dinah Washington, Lena Horne and Ertha Kitt helped her develop her own unique vocal delivery encompassing blues and rock and that she also was influenced by white rock artists like David Bowie, Mick Jagger and Janis Joplin; but, with the exception of Joplin, feels most white female vocalists are "phony." As she puts it:

"There's this clean, All-American thing that comes across in the music of most white female vocalists . . . and I don't believe that innocence is actually there. If you're going to sing about love, emotion, the blues, or you've hurt me so much, then let's get down to it and sing about it."

Alicia's singing style is physical as well as vocal. As she describes it: "I jump around a lot when I'm performing. Sometimes I get on my knees and beat on the floor with my fist. I really get carried away."

Alicia Bridges

JAMES BROWN

Recording company puffery generally can be taken with many grains of salt, but Polydor Records did not overstate the case in its publicity release which said James Brown "makes Horatio Alger look like an underachiever."

The success story of this superstar who started in show business at the age of eight by singing and dancing for nickels tossed by soldiers whose shoes he shined in front of the Augusta, Georgia, radio station he vowed one day to own (and did) is as spectacular as the wardrobe of five hundred suits, three hundred pairs of shoes and the fleet of six custom-made limousines he owns.

The career of the raucous rhythm and blues performer whose vocals, contortionistic acrobatics and percussive, polyrhythmic musical beat brought him the title of "Soul Brother Number One" in the 60's and 70's almost got sidetracked before it got started when conviction for car theft and breaking and entering put him in an Alto, Georgia, reform school for three years as a teenager.

But the reform took root in the heart of the black street kid who had known nothing but a life of deprivation and hustling from the time of his birth (stated variously by biographers to have been in 1928 in Pulaski, Tennessee and by Brown to have been in 1933 in Macon, Georgia), and on leaving confinement, he vowed to become a big-league baseball pitcher, an ambition scotched by a leg injury he sustained playing semi-pro ball.

He also turned to the church; he sang in a Baptist choir, taught himself to play drums, bass, piano and organ, and formed a gospel group called the Swannees, which was to become his Famous Flames. At the studios of the same WRDW that later was to become Brown's, they cut a demonstration record which attracted the attention of Syd Nathan of King Records, who signed them to a contract with his subsidiary label, Federal Records. Their first release for this company in 1956 was "Please,

Please, Please," written by Brown and John Terry; it reached No. 6 on the R & B charts and became the first of more than 20 Brown records to be million sellers. It was followed by "Try Me," which made No. 1 in 1958. But it was mostly through his pioneering of road tours for black artists and the tortuous crisscrossing of the nation for one-night stands that Brown established the reputation of being "the hardest working man in show business" and built the growing national audience which put his classic album "The James Brown Show Live at the Apollo" on the Billboard album charts for 66 weeks beginning in 1963.

He engaged in a bitter legal struggle with Nathan over artistic control of his work in which he formed his own production company and merchandised a package of his songs, including one of his biggest hits with whites, "Out of Sight," through Mercury's subsidiary, Smash. Brown went back to King Records with his having full control and made history with the international hit "Papa's Got a Brand New Bag," which sold 2,000,000 copies, won him a Grammy for Best Rhythm and Blues Record of the Year and set the wave of the future for R & B.

Striving to develop a sound distinctive from that of their contemporaries, Brown and the Flames injected grittiness, hysteria and Latin cross-rhythms at the same time Ray Charles was tempering rawness with sweetness. They inexorably pulled rhythm and blues into the mix of lowdown, funky blues and the high-flying emotional gospel of sanctified black churches. This combination became the trademark of mainstream contemporary black pop of the 70's and the primary forerunner of the Jamaican reggae and Nigerian Afro-beat styles of the 80's.

Their heavy shuffle beat treated every instrument as a drum and subordinated everything to Brown's semi-improvised, evangelistic, unconventional gospel-and-blues lyrics which shrieked with raw-throated emotion and were punctuated by acrobatic gyrations climaxing in his famed "collapse" routine in which he feigned fainting. He was covered by colorful capes and was helped offstage only to return in new, more flamboyant costumes to repeat the process three times.

When critics panned him and his works as "repetitive," writer Robert Palmer said that their comments were as banal as "attacking Africans for being overly fond of drumming." Brown never achieved a large white following, and only six of his singles ever made Billboard's Top Ten, the highest being No. 3 "I Got You (I Feel Good)" in 1965; but in his own rhythm-and-blues category he has placed 17 singles in first place and a total of 50 in the Top 10 to say nothing of his many hit albums and his concert work which earned him as much as $12,500 a night in the mid-60's when he could fill a large hall by himself, something no other R & B performer could do. His "collapse" was featured in the 1965 film "The T. A. M. I. Show," and he did sound-tracks for two movies of the 70's, "Black Caesar" and "Slaughter's Big Rip-Off." He became the first black man to win Cash Box Magazine's Male Vocalist Award, which came in 1979.

Other of his No. 1 R & B hits in addition to "I Got You" included "It's a Man's Man's Man's World" in 1966; "Cold Sweat" in 1967; "I Got the Feelin' " and "Say It Loud — I'm Black and I'm Proud" in 1968; "Give It Up or Turn It A'loose" and "Mother Popcorn (Part 1)" in 1969; "Super Bad" in 1970; "Hot Pants" and "Make It Funky" in 1971; "Talking Loud and Saying Nothing" and "Get on the Good Foot" in 1972; and "The Payback — Part I," "My Thang" and "Papa Don't Take No Mess" in 1974. He sweetened his sound with strings and vocal groups in the last of the 70's, but the disco fad prompted him to go for a harsher and more aggressive approach. His audience tired of that, however, and his first disco-oriented release, "The Payback" on Polydor, went to gold in 1974. His highest single placement since that time was "Get Up Offa That Thing," which reached No. 4 in 1976.

During the 60's Brown also became involved in politics as an exponent of black capitalism; he supported the presidential candidacy of Vice President Hubert Humphrey, entertained troops in Vietnam and Korea and toured Africa to cite his own success as an entrepreneur in the record production, music publishing and radio business (always taking pleasure in noting that the three stations he owned included Augusta's WRDW where his career started).

Then he devoted much of his time to encouraging young people to get an education and to avoid the perils of crime and drugs and donated ten percent of the proceeds of his concerts to black charities and ghetto causes. He received the commendation of President Lyndon Johnson for his multihour television appearances in Boston and Washington urging restoring of peace and an end to violence in the riots which followed the assassination of Dr. Martin Luther King, Jr. A similar performance during the Augusta race riots also was credited with minimizing the violence and damage of that outbreak.

Following Brown's comeback concert at Irving Plaza in New York City in 1980, critic Kurt Loder observed that although Brown's voice "may be muted . . . the legend — make no mistake — lives."

In 1983, Brown was inducted into the Georgia Music Hall of Fame.

James Brown and Zell Miller

BOUDLEAUX AND FELICE BRYANT

When Hank Penny talked him into switching from classical violinist with the Atlanta Civic Symphony to swinging country fiddler with his Radio Cowboys on station WSB in 1938, Boudleaux Bryant used a four-letter term to categorize that kind of music; but after almost four decades of achieving fame and fortune in writing more than 6,000 country songs, he would have to admit the four letters he should have used are "G-O-L-D."

Everything Boudleaux and his wife, Felice, have touched has turned to gold since their marriage in 1945. Called the Rogers and Hammerstein of Nashville, Tennessee, they are the undisputed champions of country songwriting. The words and music they have turned out have sold more than one quarter of a billion records and tapes ranging from all the twenty-seven hits recorded by the Everly Brothers to the internationally renowned country classic, "Rocky Top."

Their songs have been recorded not only in every style but also by every significant artist and group since the early Fifties, ranging from Eddy Arnold to Bob Dylan, the Carter Family to Lawrence Welk, Dean Martin and Elvis Presley and the Boston Pops Orchestra to the Grateful Dead. As the first professional songwriters who were not also performers to move to Nashville, they probably have contributed more successful songs to the mainstream of music coming out of Music City than any other songwriter or team of songwriters.

Born February 13, 1920, in Shellman, Georgia, Boudleaux was named for the French soldier who saved his lawyer-father's life in France in World War I. He grew up in Moultrie, Georgia, in a musical family which had its own band and paid its way to the 1934 Chicago World's Fair by performing on tours along the way. He was given a violin for his fifth Christmas and was sufficiently classically trained to join the Atlanta Symphony at the age of eighteen, but his association with Penny and his innovative country music ideas switched him from "longhair" to "hillbilly" and set him on the course which gave the world some of its most memorable songs.

He met his Italian singer-dancer-elevator operator wife while playing with a jazz group in Milwaukee. He brought her home to Moultrie, and they were playing clubs in that area when they sold their first song, "Country-Boy," to the Acuff-Rose organization in Nashville which made a hit of it with Little Jimmie Dickens.

They moved to Nashville to become $45-a-week song pluggers, and it has been rare indeed when one of their songs has not been in the charts since. They had the foresight to specify in their contract that all copyrights would revert to them after ten years, and they now have their own firm, The House of Bryant, to manage the royalties their more than one thousand published songs bring in and to merchandise the hundreds of others they have yet to release commercially. In recent years they have launched performing and recording careers of their own with several albums already released with particular success in Europe.

In 1953 they began a highly successful relationship with Carl Smith by writing his Top Ten hit, "Hey Joe," a song that gave Frankie Laine a million seller in the pop field. Eddy Arnold had hits with their "I've Been Thinking" and "Richest Man" in 1955. In 1957 they contracted to do some songs for the two singing sons of Boudleaux's barber, Ike Everly. They produced the string hits beginning with "Bye, Bye Love" and continued with "Wake Up Little Susie," "All I Have to Do Is Dream," "Bird Dog" and "Devoted to You." The Everly Brothers sold more than fifteen million recordings of Bryant songs but did not have a major hit after a contract dipute ended the relationship.

Although both write words and music, usually Boudleaux does the score and Felice supplies the lyrics. Their phenomenal string of hits includes "Raining in My Heart" by Buddy Holly, "Blue Boy" by Jim Reeves, "Let's Think About Loving" by Bob Luman, "Mexico" by Bob Moore, "My Last Date" by Skeeter Davis, "Baltimore" by Sonny James, "We Could" by Charlie Pride, "Take Me As I Am" by Mark White, "Come Live With Me" by Roy Clark, "Sweet Deceiver" and "Penny Arcade" by Christy Lane and "Hey Joe, Hey Moe" by Joe Stampley and Moe Bandy (an updating of their first hit, "Hey Joe").

"Rocky Top," which was written jointly in about ten minutes while they were taking a break from writing songs for an old folks album for Archie Campbell, was first done by Buck Owens and later by virtually every major country artist. Carly Simon and James Taylor made the Everlys' "Devoted to You" a major hit for a second time in 1978. Billboard Magazine in 1974 made a list of more than four hundred artists who have recorded Bryant songs.

Boudleaux and Felice now live in Gatlinburg, Tennessee. One of their sons is an executive with BMI, and the other runs their second publishing house, Claremont Publications, which handles songs of writers other than the Bryants.

Boudleaux Bryant

PEABO BRYSON

Peabo Bryson calls himself a "romantic ballad singer" and denies that he wants or tries to be a sex symbol; but the slender, handsome black farm boy from Mauldin, South Carolina, who now lives in a palatial mansion near Atlanta's airport, made himself a millionaire by turning on female audiences with his singing the songs he writes about love and passion while he is dressed all in white with the shirt opened to his navel and the suit adorned simply with a red handkerchief.

He hit recording gold with his second album, "Reaching for the Sky," in 1977 and has topped success with success since as both solo performer and in duet with such female stars as Natalie Cole, Roberta Flack and Melissa Manchester.

The oldest child in a farm family deserted by its father, Peabo began farm work at the age of seven to help support his grandmother, mother and siblings. His mother taught him to love music, and when only twelve he won a local talent contest in 1963 singing a song of his idol, Sam Cooke.

At fourteen he left home to join a singing group, and two years later was touring the world and recording on first the Custom and then the Bang labels with Mose Dillard and the Tex-Town Display. Impressed by Peabo's songwriting, Bang's Eddie Brisco gave him a contract, but his first single "Disco Queen," Peabo regarded as "awful," however, his first album, "Peabo," issued in 1976 hit the charts and Peabo hit the road.

After Peabo had several concerts with Natalie Cole, Capitol Records Vice President Larkin Arnold signed him with that label where his premier album, "Reaching for the Sky," earned him a Gold Record and, by his own estimate, "a couple of million dollars." His follow-up, "Crosswinds," with its hit single, "I'm So Into You," duplicated that success and put him at the top of the soul charts. Then came his "Best of Friends" duet album with Natalie Cole which set the pattern for the resurgence of duet songs, particularly those featuring Peabo.

In 1980 Peabo released the solo album, "Paradise," which resulted in a nationwide summer tour with Roberta Flack and their highly successful double duet album, "Live and More," as well as his doing the male lead vocal in Melissa Manchester's pop hit, "Lovers After All."

In 1981, he directed the production of an album compiling and reissuing all of his tracks recorded before the Capitol contract, and this album, titled "Turn the Hands of Time," also went to the top of the charts. Since that time he has devoted himself largely to concerts which always attract sell-out female audiences who often drown out opening acts with cries of "Bring on Peabo!"

Always the showman, Peabo enhances his all-white costuming by opening his concerts amid wisps of white smoke while singing the title track from his "Crosswinds" album. He establishes a cozy, almost hypnotic, rapport with his audience from the beginning and features in succession his suggestive "I'm So Into You;" his keyboard performance of his caring tribute to women, "She's a Woman;" and his powerfully moving "Feel the Fire;" and climaxes with the lazy sensuality of "Don't Touch Me."

Chicago Sun-Times critic Patricia Smith wrote in 1979 a review about his impact: "When the lights came up and the double-breasted knight was gone, everyone sat smiling in their seats for a minute. The good feeling he left was not easy to shake."

Peabo's latest release appropriately is entitled "I Am Love," which he describes as "expressing love through music" and embodying his belief that "everybody is love."

BUDDY BUIE

Buddy Buie has dedicated himself to the search for "the perfect sound" since he teamed up with Bobby Goldsboro, his hometown buddy from Dothan, Alabama, while they were students at Auburn University in 1961; and, while he continues that unrelenting quest more than two decades later, critics agree he may never come closer than he has with the music of the Atlanta Rhythm Section or the records he produces at his Studio One in Doraville, Georgia, which is regarded by musicians as one of the nation's finest recording facilities.

Buddy's name never has become a household word because his megatalents as manager, producer and songwriter have kept him in the background while the artists he directs and the songs he writes, arranges and records make the musical headlines. He managed Bobby Goldsboro until he became a superstar. He and guitarist T. R. Cobb formed the songwriting team which made Dennis Yost and the Classics IV the television and recording sensation of the 60's with such hits as "Spooky," "Stormy," "Traces" and "Everday With You Girl."

He produced such stars as Billy Joe Royal, Tommy Roe, B. J. Thomas and Roy Orbison and had more than 20 chart records in the 60's. He established his own recording company in 1970 which grew into the Studio One of today and his facilities attracted some of the finest musicians of the world. The quality of their studio sessions prompted him to mold them into a band which he dubbed the Atlanta Rhythm Section and which, by 1973, became a major act pronounced by critics as "the quintessential American band."

It was Buie who insisted that ARS shun gimmicks and flash costumes, limit recordings to no more than four minutes and concentrate instead on music which, under his guidance, evolved into a hybrid brand of British rock, traditional southern rhythm and blues and melody lines missing in other southern bands of the decade. In five years they produced hits with Buie songs like

"Doraville," "So Into You," "Imaginary Lovers," "Champagne Jam," "Georgia Rhythm" and many others to which the classification "Champagne Jam" stuck and continues to apply. Their successes ranged from an invitation to play the Carter White House to packing 61,000 fans into Georgia Tech's Grant Field for the unequalled and still-talked-about Champagne Jam of 1978. ARS popularity and demand continued unabated into the decade of the 80's.

In 1978 Buddy formed a management partnership with Arnie Geller called the Buie-Geller Organization and they established BGO Records which made it big right off with more hits from the Atlanta Rhythm Section and the discovery of Alicia Bridges whose monster single, "I Love The Nightlife," was an industry sensation. Buddy also produced Stillwater's first album which yielded the top 40 hit, "Mindbender."

Perhaps the one word best describing Buie's talents is "catalyst." He has demonstrated an unequalled ability to bring together individual talents and mold them into even-greater collective entities. He insists upon quality in all that he does and his enduring and unending passion is to achieve the "perfect sound." Those who know him are willing to bet that, if anyone ever finds it, Buddy Buie will be he.

JEAN CARN

Jazz singer Jean Carn is a big star in Washington, Philadelphia, New York, Chicago and Los Angeles, but she deliberately has kept a low profile in her hometown of Atlanta in order to be able to rear her children in virtual anonymity.

Born Sarah Perkins, she was active in chorus, band and orchestra at Washington High School and sang opera at Morris Brown College while performing in local nightclubs. She moved to California after marrying keyboardist Doug Carn where they recorded three albums for the Black Jazz label and she sang with Earth, Wind and Fire on two of their albums. After her divorce she was signed to a solo contract by Kenny Gamble and Leon Huff of Philadelphia International and became a part of the "Philadelphia Sound" which included Teddy Pendergrass and the Ojays.

Recording with jazz drummer Norman Conners, she has broadened her repertoire to a more commercial blend of rhythm and blues, pop, disco and jazz styles and her Philadelphia International albums have included such hits as "Start the Fire" and "My Love Don't Come Easy." Contending "you can boogie and become enlightened at the same time," she also has concentrated on message songs such as those emphasizing the plight of black males on her album "Shortage Of Good Men."

At the age of 34 she spends three weeks of each month on concert tours and makes her home with her three children in Atlanta.

JOSEPH A.
(COTTON) CARRIER

For more than 40 years Cotton Carrier has been an influential presence on the music scene of the State of Georgia. From the time he came to Georgia from Kentucky in 1941 to be master of ceremonies of the WSB Barn Dance to his present service as General Professional Manager of The Lowery Group of Music Publishing Companies, he has been a major contributor to the development not only of modern country music but also of popular music in general as we know it today.

Born to a banjo-playing father and an organ-playing mother on a farm near Arthur, Kentucky, Carrier decided by the time he was 16 that he had rather be known as "Cotton" than to pick the stuff and that singing and playing the mandolin, guitar and fiddle "beat working on the farm." He and some other boys his age formed a hometown hillbilly band which played at a local service station and he became confident enough in his musical ability to hitchhike around the country making a living through guest appearances on local radio stations. He later landed a permanent spot with a hillbilly group called Goober and His Kentuckians and was working as their fiddler for Station WPAD in Paducah, Kentucky, when he was hired by WSB to come to Atlanta to be fiddler and master of cermonies of its popular new Barn Dance.

Cotton became widely known through those Saturday night appearances on stages throughout the Atlanta area and worked with such popular Georgia performers as the Hoot Owl Hollow Girls, Boots Woodall, Pete Cassell, Harpo Kidwell, the Swanee River Boys, Chick Stripling, Hank Penny, James and Martha Carson and the pretty accordionist Jane Logan whom he soon made Mrs. Cotton Carrier. In addition he appeared on WSB's early morning Dixie Farm and Home Hour, mid-morning Cracker Barrel Program and the noontime Georgia Jubilee and, virtually every night, he and a group of WSB musicians would

Joseph A. (Cotton) Carrier

journey to some outlying town to do a show at a school auditorium or movie theater. He also formed his own band, the Plantation Gang, which was one of the last groups to appear on the WSB Barn Dance before it went out of existence in 1950 and at one time or another featured such well-known Georgia musicians as Dink Embry, Dean Bence, Church Franklin, Lee Roy Blanchard, Arlie Wade, Willis Hogsed and Calvin Bragg. As country music turned more to records than live performances, he also became a disc jockey and had his own popular Columbia Record Roundup on WSB every Saturday night at 11:30 p.m. and for a few years in the early 50's the "Cotton Carrier Show."

The advent of television found Cotton equal to the challenge, singing with Boots Woodall and the TV Wranglers on WAGA-TV of Atlanta. He also branched out into booking, bringing out-of-town talent to the Sports Arena and other Atlanta stages, and was responsible for Elvis Presley's first Atlanta appearance on December 2, 1955, a performance for which he and three back-up musicians received a total of $300 and about which Cotton later said he was not "overly impressed" although he did find Elvis a sincere and polite young man who "sang his heart out."

Cotton also wrote songs and his first hit was recorded in 1953, the year the Weavers made it big with a version of "On Top of Old Smoky" in which the lines of the song were alternately recited and sung. The Smith Brothers, a popular Atlanta gospel quartet, asked him to write a song in that same format for them and he produced with the smash, "I Have But One Goal," which was the first hit of Bill Lowery's fledgling music publishing firm which subsequently has grown into The Lowery Group.

When country music and musicians began gravitating to Nashville, Tennessee, in the decade of the 60's, Cotton elected to stay in Atlanta, a city with which he had fallen in love. Bill Lowery invited him to join his organization as a record promoter and the two of them developed into the team which since has produced a steady stream of blockbuster hits which have scored in all categories of the charts. He presently holds the title of general professional manager with the Lowery Group.

Fiddlin' John Carson
Courtesy of the Country Music Foundation Library and Media Center

FIDDLIN' JOHN CARSON

The music of Fiddlin' John Carson from Fannin County, Georgia, was the first of what we know today as "country music" to be broadcast by radio and recorded for the phonograph.

He and his daughter Rosa Lee, who was known as Moonshine Kate, were the first stars despite the fact that little of the fame and none of the fortunes produced in the country music industry ever were theirs.

Carson, fifty-four years old, had won the Georgia Fiddlin' Championship seven times and had a colorful reputation as a traveling performer who made a living playing and "passing the hat" when he was not working in the cotton mill, painting houses or making moonshine when he walked into the "studios" of the brand new Radio Station WSB started by The Atlanta Journal.

When he announced that he would "like to have a try at the new-fangeled contraption," Lambdin Kay obliged him; and his only pay being a snort of the engineer's whiskey, Carson performed "Little Old Log Cabin in the Lane." There being no FCC or radio logs kept at that time, the date generally is fixed at September 9, 1922. Some who disagree with this date insist that it came within the first week of the station's signing on the air on March 16, 1922, but probably it was on Carson's birthday of March 23. They point out that Carson always came back to WSB to perform on his birthdays well into the 1940's.

At any rate, it was before anyone else, and he returned soon thereafter with Ed Kincaid and Bill Badgett, two of his "cronies" as his early informal band was called, and played "Sally Goodin" and "Alabama Gals." According to The Atlanta Journal of September 21, 1922 he came back again with Rosa Lee and his wife, Jennie Nora, who was a "straw beater" to do a repeat of "Little Old Log Cabin." That performance brought him invitations to be a guest performer at the WSB Radio Booth at the Southeastern Fair in October and regularly in the studios thereafter.

The Journal reported that Carson's fame spread "to every corner of the United States where WSB is heard." His popularity inspired Polk Brockman, an Atlanta furniture dealer who had been successful in developing and merchandising "race" records for the black market for Okeh Records, to persuade Okeh President Ralph Peer to bring his recording equipment to Atlanta to record Fiddlin' John.

On June 14, 1923, in a vacant building on Nassau Street in Atlanta, Georgia, Carson cut two sides, "Little Old Log Cabin" and "The Old Hen Cackled and the Rooster's Going to Crow." Peer pronounced them "pluperfect awful" but agreed to press five hundred on a blank label for Brockman's personal use.

With Fiddlin' John hawking them from the stage of the next fiddlers' convention, Brockman promptly sold every disc. Peer immediately rushed into a major pressing on the Okeh label and invited Carson to New York to record twelve more sides.

This venture gave Okeh the cream of Carson's repertoire including the above two and "Billy in the Low Ground," "Sally Goodin," "Fare You Well, Old Joe Clark," "Nancy Rowland," "Kicking Mule," "When You and I Were Young, Maggie," "Casey Jones," "The Farmer is the Man That Feeds Them All," "You Will Never Miss Your Mother Until She's Gone," "Be Kind to a Man When He is Down," "Papa's Billy Goat," and "Tom Watson Special." The next year he had Rosa Lee and his classic and personal favorite, "Little Mary Phagan," which he wrote in commemoration of the infamous murder-lynching case.

Carson's grandson and namesake, John Carson, who was an All-American football player at The University of Georgia, has a list of over 150 songs written by Fiddlin' John, and his recordings for both Okeh and RCA number more than 300. Only nine of those were ever copyrighted because neither John nor Rosa Lee could read music and had to rely on others to transcribe their works, mostly WSB staff pianist Irene Spain, who later said she was embarrassed by some of the "ugly words" of Carson's lyrics.

He got into several copyright disputes with Okeh Records with Gid and Gordon Tanner, and particularly with Irene's stepfather, the blind, hymn-singing preacher Andy Jenkins, when both of them claimed to be the author of the hit ballad "Floyd Collins." Carson sold all his copyrights for a pittance shortly before he died.

58

From the age of three, Rosa Lee performed with her father, first as a buck dancer and then later as a guitar and banjo player. She adopted the name "Moonshine Kate" at the suggestion of the record company after she and Fiddlin' John recorded the popular "Corn Liquor Still in Georgia." The youngest of Carson's ten children, she was quiet, shy and totally opposite to the brassy wench she played on stage and in recordings. Of all the talented and shifting performers who made up Carson's bands, first the "Cronies" and at the height of his recording popularity, the "Virginia Reelers," she was his favorite, and it was to her that he left the treasured violin reputedly made by the son of Stradivari; at the age of ten, Carson had inherited it from his father.

Carson and his daughter apparently started the tradition of country stars' endorsing and performing for political personalities. They entertained audiences for Tom Watson in his 1920 senate campaign, for Gene Talmadge in all his campaigns and for Herman Talmadge in his first campaign for governor. Herman Talmadge rewarded him with a job as elevator operator and the title of "Elevator Commissioner" in the state capitol a title which he held to his death.

Rosa Lee married her childhood sweetheart, Wayne Johnson, and they retired after respective careers with the City of Atlanta and in business to live on Lake Seminole near Donalsonville in southwest Georgia. Reminiscing about her father, she said he never objected to being called a "hillbilly" rather than "country."

Reports dispute whether Fiddlin' John was paid for each record he sold or was on salary from the record companies with which he worked, but either way he realized very little of the wealth he earned for the companies or the promoters of his appearances throughout the United States. He died almost penniless at the age of eighty-one in Atlanta on December 11, 1949.

Phil Walden, founder of Capricorn Records, discoverer of Otis Redding, developer of The Allman Brothers Band and other southern rock groups. From Macon, Walden now lives in Nashville, Tennessee and has helped start Triad Records.

JAMES AND MARTHA CARSON

Few remember them today because they made their last recording together in 1950 and divorced in 1951, but during the 1940's James and Martha Carson were the sweethearts of country music when they started as "James and Martha" the mandolin-guitar gospel-singing duet on the WSB Barn Dance in Atlanta.

Their recordings made James' composition, "Man of Galilee," a gospel hit; "The Sweetest Gift, a Mother's Smile," a bluegrass standard; and "He Will Set Your Fields on Fire," a gospel classic.

They rank only behind the Louvins and The Blue Sky Boys as one of the greatest country duets of the early years, and Martha went on to greater fame as a solo performer on the Grand Ole Opry and in posh supper clubs like that of the Waldorf Astoria in New York City and as the writer of "Satisfied" and more than one hundred other songs of the gospel genre.

Both natives of Kentucky — he born James William Roberts, February 18, 1918, near Richmond, the son of Fiddling Doc Roberts, she born Irene Amburgey, May 19, 1921, at Neon, one of the singing Amburgey sisters, they met while performing on the WLAP Lexington Morning Roundup. He followed her as she and her sisters became first the Coon Creek Girls on the CBS Renfro Valley Barndance and then the Hoot Owl Holler Girls on the WSB Barn Dance in Atlanta.

Hank Penny got around WSB's rule against married performers by changing Robert's last name to Carson, taking Irene's performing name of "Marthie," and billing them as "James and Martha — The Barn Dance Sweethearts." They were an instant and enduring success for ten years and made a number of recordings for RCA, White Church, and Capitol labels while in Atlanta including Hank Williams' "I'm Going to Sing, Sing, Sing," Albert Brumley's "I'll Fly Away" and James' "Budded on Earth To Bloom in Heaven."

61

James moved on to join Wilma Lee and Stoney Cooper's Clinch Mountain Clan, the Masters Family and Cas Walker. Martha recorded with her sisters as the Amber Sisters and then pursued a career as a single gospel and country singer who produced in addition to "Satisfied" such hits as "I'm Gonna Walk and Talk With My Lord," "Let the Light Shine on Me," "Lazarus," "Ole Blind Barnabus," "It Takes a Lot of Lovin'," and "I Can't Stand Up Alone." Both have remarried and have two children each. Martha lives in Nashville, Tennessee, and James in Lexington, Kentucky.

Martha Carson
Courtesy of the Country Music Foundation Library and Media Center

RAY CHARLES

It was the unspoken consensus of the Georgia General Assembly when it voted in 1979 to make the Hoagy Carmichael-Charles Gorrell tune "Georgia on My Mind" the official state song that its first performance as such would be by Ray Charles, the black musician born in Albany, Georgia.

He had sung that song in every concert he had played since first recording it, but Ray Charles probably had contributed as much to the integration of American society through his pioneering in the erasing of racial boundaries in music as any civil rights leader through confrontations and demonstrations.

He readily accepted the invitation to sing and on March 7, 1979, received a thundering ovation when he officially introduced Georgians to their new state song in a performance at the State Capitol. This honor came almost a quarter of a century after he recorded his first great hit song, "I Got a Woman," in the studios of Atlanta's radio station WGST.

It had been a long, hard road of struggle and success, tragedy and triumph for Charles, who was born Ray Charles Robinson on September 23, 1930, the son of an automobile mechanic who died when Ray was ten and of a strong-minded mother who took in washing; she died when he was fifteen.

He was blinded by glaucoma when he was six after the family moved to Greenville, Florida, and two of his most vivid sighted memories are of the horror of seeing his younger brother drown in one of his mother's washtubs and of the pleasure of learning his first piano chords from Wylie Pittman. Pittman was a neighbor who ran a general store in which he kept a piano on which he played Southern boogie and a juke box on which he played the "race" records of Big Boy Crudup, Tampa Red, Blind Boy Fuller and Big Joe Turner and the swing recordings of Duke Ellington, Count Basie and Benny Goodman. Drumming into his head that he was "blind, not stupid," Charles' mother insisted that he learn to do everything a sighted child would do, including chopping

Ray Charles

wood, and enrolled him in the St. Augustine School for the Deaf and Blind at the age of seven where he learned to read, write and play music by Braille as well as to make brooms and mops and to tool leather billfolds and belts.

He quickly decided he preferred music to crafts as a life's calling and mastered the piano, organ, alto clarinet and trumpet to the point that, by his early teens, he was professionally proficient in music ranging from Chopin and Sibelius to Artie Shaw and Art Tatum. He refused to eat in grief over his mother's death, but after being force-fed by friends who convinced him his mother would want him to carry on, he lied about his age to get a union card and began playing in clubs around Florida until he saved $600 which he used to move as far away as he could get, Seattle, Washington, where at the age of 17 he won a talent contest and formed a trio to play a regular gig at the Elks Club.

He dropped his last name to avoid confusion with that of the fighter Sugar Ray Robinson and established a reputation for himself as an emulator of the music of his idol Nat "King" Cole. It was during the teen period of his career that he became hooked on heroin which turned into a 20-year habit culminating in his arrest on federal drug charges in 1965 and a year-long period of enforced probation and hospitalization in which he kicked it for good.

Swingtime Records put him under contract in 1949, and he moved to Los Angeles, where he debuted with "Confession Blues," which, like a number of its successors, did little until he hit with a Top 10 Rhythm and Blues number "Baby, Let Me Hold Your Hand" in 1951. He went on the road with Lowell Fulson, put together a band for Ruth Brown and played briefly for Moms Mabley before going to New Orleans in 1953. Here he joined up with bluesman Eddie Jones, who was known as Guitar Slim, an unsophisticated primitive for whom Ray arranged and then backed on his million-selling blues classic, "The Things That I Used To Do," for Specialty Records, which started him on the development of the musical identity that was to bring him subsequent success. Atlantic Records, which bought his contract in 1952, recorded him in New York that year on the boogie-woogie classic "Mess Around," the novelty number "It Should've Been Me;" and the blues tunes "Losing Hand," "Funny" and Fulson's "Sinner's Prayer." The next year Atlantic Records went to New Orleans to do a series of Ray Charles' originals, including the single "Don't You Know" and a moving version of Guitar Slim's "Feelin' Sad."

But they were preludes to the 1955 recording in Atlanta of "I Got a Woman" in which Charles broke into his new style of gospel-based piano topped by the exuberance and earthiness of his full-throated raspy baritone punctuated with falsetto shrieks. This attracted the attention of both black and white audiences and brought the protest of blues singer Big Bill Bronzey who took him to task for blending gospel and blues and declared "He's crying sanctified."

From that time on his name was constantly on the R & B and pop charts, and he had such acclaimed singles as "Blackjack," "Come Back," "Fool for You," "Greenbacks," "This Little Girl of Mine," "Drown in My Own Tears," "Hallelujah, I Love You So," "Lonely Avenue," "Mary Ann," "What Would I Do Without You," "Right Time" and "What'd I Say," which critics agree was one of the most sensual and explosive singles of the modern pop-rock era.

He did two standing room only concerts at Carnegie Hall in 1963 and became popular in concerts and appearances at theaters, clubs and jazz festivals throughout the nation. He won the first of his 10 Grammys also in 1963 for the song "Busted" as the Best Rhythm and Blues Recording of the Year. His albums were consistent best sellers throughout the late 50's and 60's, including "Yes, Indeed" and "At Newport" in 1958, "What'd I Say" in 1959, "In Person" in 1960, "Dedicated to You" and "Genius + Soul = Jazz" in 1961, "Modern Sounds," "The Ray Charles Story" and "Greatest Hits" in 1962, "Great Ray Charles" and "Recipe for Soul" in 1963 and "Sweet and Sour Tears" in 1964.

The gospel genesis of "I Got a Woman" started Charles on an evolution of assimilation of parts of all music forms from blues, gospel and funk to pop standards and jazz into what was to become his own unique brand of soul. The Raelettes, the back-up group of five females, became his choir, and a 17-piece band added orchestral fullness as he embarked upon tempering rawness with sweetness at the same time that James Brown was going in the other direction by injecting grittiness and hysteria.

Charles completed the dimension and added further to the criticism of the purists when he moved over into country and western when he shifted his contract to ABC-Paramount. Then he came out in 1962 with the three big hits "You Don't Know Me," "You Are My Sunshine" and "I Can't Stop Loving You," the latter of which went to No. 1, earned Gold and Platinum Records and ultimately sold more than 3,000,000 copies. (It was also during this period that "Georgia on My Mind" was first recorded and released and became a standard of all Charles' concert programs.)

From then on country and western songs were a regular part of his repertoire, and none of his albums was released thereafter without one of these songs. To those who complained, he responded that he listened to the Grand Ole Opry as a child and loved country music because "It's kind of like the blues" and the "lyrics are so plain . . . even a four-year-old can understand what you're singing."

By adding his own interpretations and stylings to the various forms of music, Charles, in effect, made it acceptable for black people to sing country and western music and white people to appreciate soul; thus he paved the way for black country singers like Charley Pride and white soul singers like Joe Cocker. (Ray always avoided racial controversy and once told Dr. Martin Luther King, Jr., he would give concerts and raise money for him but would not march or go to jail for him. He notes he was singing protest songs like "You're in for a Big Surprise" long before "black is beautiful songs came along.")

His singles hits of the 60's and 70's included "Sticks and Stones," "Hit the Road, Jack," "Them That's Got," "Ruby," "I've Got News for You," "Mint Julep," "Busted," "Don't Set Me Free," "No One," "Your Cheating Heart," "Take These Chains From My Heart," "Crying' Time," "Together Again," "Let's Get Stoned" (which went to No. 1), "Here We Go Again," "Don't Change on Me" and "Feel So Bad." An excellent example of his many multi-style albums was "True to Life," which included soul/country versions of the songs "The Jealous Kind" and "I Can See Clearly Now." At the end of the decade he left ABC and reaffiliated with Atlantic.

He has appeared as guest on every television program of consequence, including Public Broadcasting System's acclaimed country music show, "Austin City Limits." A millionaire, he also established his own music publishing firm and issued records under his own labels, Tangerine and Crossover; he purchased two jet planes to get himself and his company to an average of 300

67

concert appearances they make each year and he bought a $300,000 home overlooking the Pacific Ocean he cannot see, where he lives with his second wife and three sons (he also has a grown daughter by an earlier marriage).

In addition to his 10 Grammys, he has five consecutive awards as Top Male Vocalist in the International Jazz Critics' Poll conducted by Down Beat Magazine and a Bronze Medallion from the Government of France, a country where his concerts always attract SRO audiences.

Perhaps no modern singer and his success have been more analyzed than Charles and his phenomenal accomplishment of having sold more than 200 million records embracing all media except classical. Georgia historian Bernice McCullar said his music draws people because of "the pain, the misery, often the despair that comes through," and the foremost jazz critic, Whitney Balliett, maintains that Charles is "revered by every class, color and creed, perhaps because he touches the listeners' emotions with his voice."

While agreeing that he has "known sheer agony" and has been through "quite a bit of poverty and all kinds of hassles," Charles thinks of himself "as a musician who enjoys all kinds of music," but admits that he does "try to bring out my soul so people can understand what I am." He says he does not choose his songs because of their categories but on the basis of whether he likes them and feels there are ways he "can enhance . . . put myself into" them. He quite often turns down songs he "doesn't feel," pointing out he declined an offer of $25,000 and half the rights to do the title song of the movie "Walk on the Wild Side" because it "didn't feel right to him."

He laughs at the jokes about and parodies of his image and playing style — eyes hidden by dark glasses, stomping of the feet and rocking back and forth with the rhythm of his music — and he turns aside the assessment of Frank Sinatra that he is "the only genius in our profession" by saying "Art Tatum — he was a genius. And Einstein. Not me." But he adds that he does intend to "keep singing until the people tell me it's time for me to go out to pasture."

ALBERT COLEMAN

Cosmopolitan is the only word adequate to describe the breadth of the musical genius and the scope of the personal experience of Albert Coleman. The originator and conductor of the Atlanta Pops Orchestra, he has given almost four decades of his life to the single-minded pursuit of his goal to make beautiful music available without cost for the appreciation and edification of the masses.

Coleman is a true Renaissance man of music; his life's story is worthy of a Boris Pasternak novel, and although his baton has directed many of the finest symphony orchestras of the world and his electric musical accomplishments span the spectrum from classics to country, the acclaim he has received has far exceeded the meager financial rewards his great talents have earned.

Coleman was born Alfred Emil Emmanuel Crosner in 1911 in Paris, France, the son of a French musician named Rene and a beautiful Italian bareback horse rider named Carolina who performed together on the vaudeville stages of South America and in the circus rings of Europe. He was taught the violin by his father, performed with the troupe from the age of five and escaped with his parents from Russia in the wake of the Bolshevik Revolution in 1917 by riding on the top of a train across Siberia to China.

He grew up among Russian exiles in Shanghai, where he mastered the Russian, Chinese and English languages in addition to his native French and came under the tutelage of the conductor of the Shanghai Symphony Orchestra, in which he played the violin. He was sent back to France to study violin and conducting at the Paris Conservatory; but when his father died in Saigon, French Indochina, when Albert was 14, he formed a dance orchestra, in which he played drums, saxophone and violin, to supplement his mother's income as a language teacher.

His engagements took them throughout the Orient, and at the age of 21, he was guest conductor of the Sydney, Australia,

(left) Albert Coleman celebrates his best selling album "Just Hooked on Country" with Bill Lowery and Lt. Governor Zell Miller

Symphony Orchestra. At the age of 22, he became music conductor for the A. B. Marcus Show, a Ziegfeld type of touring company with which he worked for the next 12 years, in the Far East and around the world, including a visit to Atlanta, where he was playing at the Roxy Theater in 1939 when the premiere of "Gone With the Wind" was held next door at Loew's Grand Theater. His performances took him to Australia, New Zealand, Fiji, Hawaii, the Philippines, China, Japan, Hong Kong, Java, Borneo, the Malay States, Burma, India and South Africa.

He and his mother escaped from Singapore in advance of the Japanese invasion in 1941 and went first to Mexico and then to Canada, where he met his wife, ballerina Gwnnyth Moore. They were married in Atlanta, where he accepted a position as music director of radio station WSB in 1945, a post he held for three years. When he became an American citizen in Atlanta on January 28, 1948, he petitioned at the time for his name to be changed to Albert Coleman. He has made his home there since, and his daughter and son were born there.

He conducted four programs a day on WSB, including a very popular midnight show on which he played the violin while other staffers played the organ and read poetry; and, as part of the Station's promotional activities, he established a community orchestra and held the first of Atlanta's pop concerts at Emory University in 1945.

The next year he gave a similar concert at Fort McClellan, Alabama, and in 1947 began the yearly summer series of free public pop concerts under his baton which continued until 1976 under the joint financial sponsorship of the City of Atlanta, the Atlanta Federation of Musicians and the Fox Theater until the concerts moved outdoors to Chastain Park. Coleman's music organization, which at its zenith was composed of 55 musicians and a chorus of 30 voices, took the name Atlanta Pops Orchestra, drew SRO audiences at the Fox and crowds up to 10,000 at Chastain and attracted as many as 200 audition requests a year from aspiring young Georgia musicians. The free programs enjoyed the support of Atlanta Mayors William B. Hartsfield, Ivan Allen, Jr., and Sam Massell, but were discontinued on a series basis when Mayor Maynard Jackson withdrew the city's $6,000-a-year subsidy in favor of increased support for the Atlanta Symphony Orchestra in 1976. This action resulted in strained relations between Coleman and ASO conductor Robert

71

Shaw which often spilled over into print. The orchestra continues to perform for conventions like that of the National Conference of State Legislatures in 1981 and for July 4th and Georgia Music Week Concerts at Stone Mountain Park.

Because the pops concerts were not planned to be money makers, Coleman never received more than minimum compensation for his services and found it necessary to book talent, work as radio disc jockey, conduct hotel and nightclub orchestras, play as session and back-up musician in Atlanta and Nashville recording studios and make appearances as guest conductor for more than 60 symphony orchestras around the nation ranging from Almogordo to Wichita. He conducted orchestras for Atlanta's Theater Under the Stars; for the Southern, Civic and Ruth Mitchell Ballets of Atlanta; for two southeastern tours by Henry Mancini; for Chet Atkins' European tour; for the WSB-TV 25th Anniversary Silver Gala; and for television specials for Kraft, Bob Hope and Ed Sullivan. He recorded for RCA, including the "Music City Pops" album in 1971, which was highly praised for its combination of country music and the big band sound; and, in 1983, he and Atlanta music publisher Bill Lowery issued a country album which was nominated for a Grammy titled "Just Hooked on Country." It was patterned after the smash "Hooked on Classics" album done by the Royal Philharmonic Orchestra.

Although now a septuagenarian, Coleman has made only no concession to age. His French accent is as thick as ever, and his hopes for a long life are buoyed by the fact that his mother still is alive and active at the age of 102. He is active in the promotion of Georgia's growing music industry and reassembles his Pops Orchestra whenever he can obtain funding for the performance of his acclaimed versions of music running the gamut from rock to Rachmaninoff.

ARTHUR CONLEY

There is no telling how far Arthur Conley, a soul singer born in Atlanta, Georgia, on January 4, 1946, might have gone had his manager, the late Otis Redding, not perished in a plane crash just as Conley's career was taking off.

Conley became Redding's protege in 1967 after Redding heard one of his demonstration records and told his own manager, Phil Walden, that he was "the most dynamic young talent I've ever heard." He recorded him on his own Jotis label and produced the single, "Sweet Soul Music," which was distributed by Atlantic Records to become a Gold Record. The fact that it went to the top of the charts in England, Holland, the Philippines and Puerto Rico brought him an enthusiastic European tour.

Later that year Redding produced him back on the charts with two more singles, "Shake, Rattle and Roll" and "Whole Lotta Woman." His career began to lose momentum with Redding's tragic death, although he did have lesser hits with "Funky Street," "People Sure Act Funny" and "Dora's Love Soul Shack" in 1968, his version of the Beatles' "Ob-La-Di, Ob-La-Da" in 1969 and "God Bless" in 1970.

JOHNNY DARRELL

Music stars who were discovered in drugstores have nothing on country music singer and songwriter Johnny Darrell of Marietta, Georgia. He was discovered by United Artists' producer Kelso Herstin while he was working as manager of the Holiday Inn just off Music Row in Nashville.

His career as a recording artist was launched with the first of many successful versions of Curley Putnam's classic, "Green, Green Grass of Home," on the Cartwheel label.

While his successes have not been as spectacular as those of some of his contemporaries who expanded the "Nashville Sound" in the mid-Sixties, Darrell proved his ear for hit songs with messages by also being the first to record "Ruby, Don't Take Your Love To Town" (which he had to fight to do because of its controversial subject matter), "The Son of Hickory Holler's Tramp," "With Pen in Hand" and others which were later turned into hits by bigger names.

His talent was early recognized by Kris Kristofferson himself who produced him on six sides for Monument Records in 1972 after he recorded ten albums for United Artists between 1965 and 1969. He also worked on the West Coast with Clarence White of the Byrds, Rusty Young of Poco, Mike Potts of Bread and other leaders in the fusion of country, pop and rock styles of the time.

Johnny, who was born in Muscadine, Alabama, grew up in Marietta and Atlanta. He recorded two highly acclaimed albums for Capricorn Records of Macon, "Water Glass Full of Whiskey," and "Rice Colored Gin." Critics praise his voice as one "which transcends country, pop and rock . . . (and) carries the full emotions of the songs as they were written."

MAC DAVIS

Despite the fact that his adoring stepfather, the late Georgia Public Service Commissioner Bill Kimbrough, set him up with a job with the State Board of Probation on the top floor of the State Capitol, Mac Davis could not stay away from the swimming pool at Emory University where he banged on the bongo drums and twanged on his guitar to attract girls. In so doing, he perfected the free-wheeling, crossover rock-pop-country musical style which made him one of the most popular and successful songwriters and performers from the late 60's to present.

He writes songs and makes jokes about the Texas roots dating from his birth in Lubbock on January 21, 1941 but it was in Georgia that he honed his easy-going "good-ole-boy" manner into the sharp talents of the all-around entertainer who has achieved stardom as the writer and singer of hit songs, the host of his own and special television programs, a headliner at Las Vegas and an actor in major movies.

From growing up as a choirboy whose idols were Elvis Presley and Buddy Holly, he forsook government employment for a rock group he and his Emory buddies formed called the Zots. They made a reputation for hot licks in the Atlanta area teen hangouts of Misty Waters and Knotty Pines. He was seventeen when he sold his first song, "The Phantom Strikes Again." He later received $2.42 in recording royalties.

He gave up rocking-and-rolling in 1961 to take a job as Atlanta regional manager for Vee Jay Records and moved to a similar position with Liberty (now United Artists) Records in 1965. Later he was promoted to head Metric Music, its musical publishing operation in Hollywood. There he began to tout the backlog of songs he had written over the years. He scored in 1967-68 when Lou Rawls and Glen Campbell made the charts with "You're Good To Me" and "Within My Memory" respectively. Elvis Presley recorded his "A Little Less Conversation" in

1968 which prompted Colonel Tom Parker to rub his curly locks "for luck" and Elvis to write some new songs for him.

He gave Presley three hits in 1969-70 — "In The Ghetto," "Memories" and "Don't Cry, Darling" — and did music for Elvis' first television special and two of his movies. He then penned "Friend, Lover, Woman and Wife" and "Daddy's Little Man" for O. C. Smith, "Watching Scotty Grow" for Bobby Goldsboro and "Something's Burning" for Kenny Rogers and The First Edition.

His career sky-rocketed in the early 70's when he signed with Columbia and scored with successive Gold Records of "Baby, Don't Get Hooked On Me," "I Believe in Music" (which became a pop standard recorded by more than fifty different artists), "Stop and Smell the Roses," and "One Hell Of A Woman." He made a series of best-selling albums around those singles and most of his pop hits also made the country lists.

He had his own television show on NBC, made guest appearances on all the major talk and variety programs from Johnny Carson down and became a regular headliner in Las Vegas. He was named Country Music Association Entertainer of the year, hosting the CMA Annual Awards telecast for two consecutive years, and received the People's Choice Award for Favorite Male Entertainer.

He was still putting hits in the country charts when his pops successes slowed and they included "I Still Love You," "Forever Lovers," and "Picking Up Pieces Of My Life." The latter was an autobiographical song, as was "Watching Scotty Grow," written about his son.

He began doing a number of highly rated television specials in the mid-70's and late in the decade moved to Casablanca Records which put him back in the Top Ten in 1980 with the hit single "It's Hard To Be Humble," and earned him a Gold Record for the album by the same name. Later in the 80's he added two more top singles "Lets' Keep it This Way," and "Texas In My Rear View Mirror," his own composition. Next came singles successes with "Hooked on Music" and "You're My Bestest Friend" and a top selling album "Midnight Crazy." To date he has done three well-received movies: "North Dallas Forty," "Cheaper To Keep Her" and "The Sting II."

Critics dispute his classification and, while most tend to put him in the country and western category, he contends one "can't put a label on my music" because it contains "a little bit of everything." He thinks his music appeals more to pop audiences old as well as young. Of all his work, he prefers to do nightclub acts where he can improvise songs from titles suggested by members of his audience.

Mac Davis

MATTIWILDA DOBBS

Mattiwilda Dobbs, the product of one of the most distinguished and respected black families of Georgia and the nation, often is credited with doing for blacks in opera what Jackie Robinson did for them in professional baseball.

The daughter of John Wesley Dobbs, the wealthy black entrepreneur who was the acknowledged head of black society in segregated Atlanta and one of the early leaders and officers in the National Association for the Advancement of Colored People, Mattiwilda graduated from Spelman College and studied voice for four years in New York where her talent won for her the John Hay Whitney Fellowship to study in Paris. She went on to triumph in the prestigious Geneva Competition which resulted in an audition at La Scala in Milan, Italy, and the role of Elvia in Rossini's "Italian Woman in Algiers" which brought her glowing reviews. She was acclaimed throughout Europe prior to returning to the United States for an American debut in San Francisco in 1955, one year after the school desegregation decision of the U. S. Supreme Court, and subsequently became one of the first black persons to sing with the Metropolitan Opera in New York City.

Her voice received the highest critical praise wherever she performed and her concert tours took her throughout the world, including Sweden, where she met her husband, Swedish Government Official Bengt Janzon, and made her home for 18 years following their marriage. She returned home for a second time in 1975 to hold a successive series of voice professorships at Spelman, the University of Illinois in Urbana, the University of Georgia and since 1977 at Howard University in Washington, D. C.

Although her main professional activity now is teaching rather than performing, she continues to give four or five concerts a year and to regard Atlanta as her home. In November of 1983 she was presented the J. Weldon Johnson Award at the Annual NAACP

Freedom Fund Dinner in Atlanta in recognition of her 35 years of stellar achievements in the arts and her contributions to eliminating racial barriers and opening doors for talented black singers in the field of opera.

She has five sisters, all of whom are renowned college professors, and credits her success to the encouragement of her late father.

"My father said he was a believer in women's liberation because he had six daughters," she told The Atlanta Journal in one of her rare interviews. "Even though he wanted us to get married, he wanted us to have our own careers."

She also professes great pride in the accomplishments of her nephew, Maynard Jackson, who served two terms as Mayor of Atlanta and was the first black to be elected to such an office in a major southern city.

Mattiwilda Dobbs

DR. THOMAS ANDREW DORSEY

Dr. Thomas Andrew Dorsey, who grew up in Georgia and began his musical career known as "Georgia Tom" playing barrelhouse piano in one of Al Capone's Chicago speakeasies and leading Ma Rainey's jazz band, was still going strong at the age of 83 after being "whipped into shape to do the Lord's will" and becoming the world-renowned "Father of Gospel Music." He lived to see the greatest of the more than 1,000 gospel songs he wrote, "Precious Lord, Take My Hand," translated into 35 languages and sung to ovations from Paris and Sierre Leone; his life immortalized in the highly-acclaimed 1982 musical documentary film, "Say Amen, Somebody," and his achievements appropriately recognized by his induction into the Georgia, Nashville Songwriters Association and Gospel Music Association Halls of Fame and the establishment of the Thomas A. Dorsey Archives containing his collected works and memorabilia by Fisk University of Nashville, Tennessee, which conferred upon him the honorary degree of doctor of music.

Dorsey learned his religion from his Baptist minister father and the piano from his music teacher mother in Villa Rica, Georgia, where he was born July 1, 1899, and came under the influence of local blues pianists when they moved to Atlanta in 1910. He and his family relocated to Chicago during World War I where they joined the Pilgrim Baptist Church and he studied at the Chicago College of Composition and Arranging and became an agent for Paramount Records. He wrote his first religious song, "If I Don't Get There," in 1921 for which the term "gospel music" was coined to describe when it was published in "The Gospel Pearls" by the National Baptist Convention. But his musical interests were more secular at the time and, after working in Capone's establishment, he graduated to playing the piano, composing and arranging for Les Hite's Whispering Seranaders;

playing along with Fred Pollack as a sideman with Will Walker's Syncopators; forming, with Pollack, his own Wildcat's Jazz Band to back Gertrude Nix Pridgett "Ma" Rainey who recorded his "Broken Hearted Blues" and "Broken Soul Blues" for Paramount; being a dominent influence in shaping the style and career of slide guitarist Hudson "Tampa Red" Whittaker with whom he recorded the best-selling blues hit, "Tight Like That," in 1928; and writing more than 460 rhythm and blues and jazz songs.

A two-year illness beginning in 1925 brought him back to the faith of his father after a minister convinced him "the Lord has work for you" and he would "be healthy and happy and live for a long time" if he did it; and, while he worked simultaneously in the fields of gospel and music and jazz for several more years and had another hit recording with the "hokum" record, "Terrible Operation Blues," done with Jane Lucas in 1930, he was one of the few to welcome Mahalia Jackson to Chicago from New Orleans in 1929 and joined with Fellow Composer Theodore R. Frye to form the Dorsey Trio which was the first group to call itself "gospel singers." In 1931 he and Frye organized the first black church gospel choir in Chicago at Ebernezer Baptist Church which, as Mahalia later recalled, brought objections from "colored ministers . . . (who) didn't like the hand-clapping and the stomping and . . . said we were bringing jazz into the church and it wasn't dignified."

But the Dorsey style of combining Baptist lyrics with sanctified beat which previously had been limited to black holiness congregations caught on and in 1932 he was appointed choral director of his own Pilgrim Baptist Church, a post he continues to hold as well as that of assistant pastor to which he was named after his subsequent ordination. Discouraged by his own efforts to publish and sell his songs through the old method of peddled "song sheets" and dissatisfied with the treatment given composers of "race" music by the music publishing industry, Dorsey became the first independent publisher of black gospel music with the establishment of the Dorsey House of Music in Chicago in 1932. He also founded and became President of the National Convention of Gospel Choirs and Choruses and, because his own light voice was not suited for the gospel sound, he established the pattern for instrumental accompaniment of gospel songs previously done a capella by hiring Chicago Singer Rebecca Tolbert

81

to sing his songs as he played them on the piano, setting the style for such well-known gospel pianists as Roberta Martin, Evelyn Gay, Curtis Dublin and Herbert Pickard. Additionally, he was the originator of black music concerts, the first being his "Battle of Song" between Roberta and Sally (not related) Martin in Chicago in 1936.

He wrote his classic and most famous song, "Precious Lord," in the grief following the death of his first wife in childbirth in 1932 and it since has been recorded by such diverse artists as Mahalia Jackson, Tennessee Ernie Ford, Roy Rogers and Dale Evans and Elvis Presley and was the favorite gospel song of both Dr. Martin Luther King, Jr., who asked that it be sung at the rally he led the night before his assassination and of President Lyndon B. Johnson who requested that it be sung at his funeral. Almost equally well known is his "Peace In The Valley" which he wrote for Mahalia Jackson in 1937 after becoming her pianist in 1935, a relationship which continued until 1946, and which was made into a million-seller country hit by Red Foley and covered by the Jordanaires. Carmen Lombardo made his "My Desire" famous; Morton Downey was successful with his "When I've Done My Best"; Sister Rosetta Tharpe recorded his "Rock Me"; Brother Joe May did his "Search Me, Lord"; the Five Blind Boys popularized his "Our Father"; and others who recorded and sang his works included the Ward Singers, the Roberta Martin Singers, Dwight "Gatemouth" Moore, Sam Cooke, Jimmy Witherspoon and the Reverend James Cleveland.

Others among the more famous of his hundreds of gospel songs are "If You Ever Needed the Lord Before," "Life Can Be Beautiful," "Let Us Sing Together," "I'm Going to Live The Life I Sing About," "In The Scheme of Things," "Watching and Waiting," "I'll Tell It Wherever I Go," "Say A Little Prayer For Me," "How About You," "If You See My Savior," "If I Could Hear My Mother Pray," "I Will Put My Trust In The Lord," "The Lord Has Laid His Hands On Me," "Stand By Me" and "We Will Meet Him In The Sweet By And By." He recorded a few of his songs in the early 30's but they mostly were done by others and it was not until 1980 that he did his first album as a solo performer, "The Maestro Sings His Masterpieces." However, he has so dominated the field that, during the 40's and 50's, all gospel songs were referred to as "Dorseys."

One must differentiate between spirituals which are handed-down religious folk songs and gospel songs which are contemporary religious music composed in the style set by Dorsey. While he was an admirer of the hymns done by Dr. Charles A. Tindley of Philadelphia whom he called his "Idol," Dorsey was the first to combine the sensitivity of black audience' demands and reactions, the sincerity and religiosity of Tindley's style, his own autobiographical religious experience and compelling rhythms, riffs and vocal stylings out of the R & B and jazz genres into songs which went back to the roots of black religion and culture. He was the first to organize and sophisticate the "call and response" technique of singing introduced into this country by African slaves and to employ the "closed" harmonic sound of black singing which presents all notes of chords in condensed, high sounds. He also established the differentiations among "slow," "without rhythm" and "fast" gospel songs — classic examples being his slow "Peace In The Valley," his fast "If You Ever Needed The Lord Before" and his without rhythm "Precious Lord, Take My Hand." It is a source of wry amusement to him that many of his "slow" and "without rhythm" songs have become so anglicized that they are used as opening "hymns" at Ku Klux Klan rallies and other segregated, racist functions.

Dorsey's biographer, Ruth Smith, called him a "Twentieth Century David," explaining that "As David sang and played in the courts of Saul, the king, so does Dorsey sing and play before the ministers and their congregations that they might be relieved of the evil that God has suffered to befall them because of their waywardness."

In October 1979, he was the first black elected to the Nashville Songwriters Association's International Hall of Fame. In December 1980 Operation Push highlighted its Jubilee Celebration with the presentation to him of its Push Par Excellent Award. In September 1981 his native Georgia honored him with election to the Georgia Music Hall of Fame; in March 1982 he was the first black elected to the Gospel Music Association's Living Hall of Fame; in August 1982 the Thomas A. Dorsey Archives were opened at Fisk University where his collection joined those of W. C. Handy, George Gershwin and the Jubilee Singers; in September 1982 he was inducted into the New York City Songwriters Hall of Fame; and in October 1982 the world premiere was held of George Nierenberg's film about him and his gospel-music contemporaries, "Say Amen, Somebody," as part of the New York Film Festival.

In the early 80's he formed the Dorsey Gospel Team with educator Dr. Clayton Hannah and music arranger Gregory Cooper to tour the nation to present programs of his works, saying "you've got to do something to live," and to present his rebuttal to current interpretations of his songs which he says have "junked them up." Summing up his life, he says all his work has been "from God, for God and for his people."

84   **Dr. Thomas Dorsey**

PETE DRAKE

To put food in the mouths of his wife and six children, Roddis Franklin "Pete" Drake, the son of a Georgia Baptist minister who gave up an Atlanta bread route for the recording studios of Nashville, literally taught the pedal steel guitar to talk.

Pete Drake, more than any other individual, created a resurgence of use on that instrument in both country and pop music to the extent that he played in thirty-eight of the recording sessions of forty-eight BMI award-winning songs for 1966, and probably is more in demand as a back-up musician than any artist today.

Not only does he have a Gold Record for his own 1964 hit, "Forever," but he also has backed an astounding list of hits for others ranging from Tammy Wynette's "Stand By Your Man" to Bob Dylan's "Lay, Lady, Lay" to albums for Beatles' George Harrision and Ringo Starr.

His Stop Records, Pete's Place Recording Studio and Window Music Publishing Company are among the busiest in Music City.

Born in Augusta on October 8, 1932, and reared in Atlanta, Pete bought his first steel guitar from a pawn shop for $33.00 and taught himself to play it in the style of Jerry Byrd while still in his teens. He built his own pedal steel guitar and formed his first band, Sons of the South, composed of the incredible fledging talents of himself, Jack Greene, Dory Kershaw, Roger Miller, Jerry Reed and Joe South.

Moving to Nashville on the encouragement of Egyptian Ballroom owner Kathleen Jackson, he responded to rebuffs from recording artists who wanted "string sections" by developing techniques for duplication of all string sounds on the steel guitar, making himself "the cheapest string section in Nashville." He backed Roy Druskey's hit, "I Don't Believe You Love Me Anymore," and followed it with George Hamilton IV's smash "Before This Day Ends."

Then following through on an idea born when watching some

85

old Alvino Rey films, he developed a mouth device which permitted him to speak words through the amplified strings of the steel guitar. Its debut created a sensation at the Grand Ole Opry for which he subsequently wrote and recorded its theme "For Pete's Sake." His albums were big successes and he employed the technique for the hits of Roger Miller, "Lock, Stock, and Teardrops," and Jim Reeves, "I've Enjoyed As Much of This As I Can Stand." His work won for him the Cashbox "Instrumentalist of the Year" Award in 1964 and Record World's "Fastest Climbing Instrumentalist of the Year" and "Number Two Most Programmed Instrumentalist of the Year" Awards in 1964 and 1969 respectively.

Both Bob Dylan and Joan Baez asked for him to work on the three albums they each recorded in Nashville, including Dylan's "Nashville Skyline" and Baez' "David's Album." Ringo Starr came to Nashville to do his "Beaucoups of Blues" album with him and George Harrison invited him to England to do his "All Things Must Pass" album with him there.

In addition, he did back-up work for the hits of Lynn Anderson with "Rose Garden," Charlie Rich with "Behind Closed Doors" and Johnny Rodriguez with "Pass Me By." He recorded a classic series of albums with Grand Ole Opry veterans like Ernest Tubb, Charlie Louvin and Jan Howard.

The list of stars with whom he has worked sounds like a Who's Who of pop and country ranging from Elvis Presley, Buffy Sainte Marie and Perry Como to George Jones, Marty Robbins and Bill Anderson. But he is proudest of creating the popular new sound of the steel guitar which he calls "the most soulful of all instruments" and warns "if you don't want to get hurt, don't listen to it."

DIXIE DREGS

It looked as if the musical dreams of classmates Steve Morse and Andy West were dashed for good when Steve was expelled from Richmond Academy in Augusta, Georgia, in the early 70's for refusing to cut his long hair, but Morse met two more talented musicians in Rod Morgenstein and Allen Sloan when he went to the University of Miami; and they, with West, formed the Dixie Dregs Band in 1972 which broke out of the pack of bands flourishing in that decade with a no-vocals, all-instrumental sound similar to that of the Mahavishnu Orchestra which defied labeling and has been described variously as progressive jazz, rock, country and even classical music.

Guitarist Morse and bassist West called their original high school group "Dixie Grit," but changed the "Grit" to "Dregs" when they reorganized in reference to their being all that was left. Morgenstein became the new drummer, Sloan the electric violinist and Steve Davidowski the keyboardist doubling on alto and soprano saxophone. They were playing in a nightclub in Macon, Georgia, in 1977 when Phil Walden of Capricorn Records, the man who made the Allman Brothers Band famous, caught their act and signed them to a contract. At the same time Twiggs Lyndon, who had worked with Little Richard, Otis Redding and the Allmans, signed on as their road manager.

The Dregs produced their first album for Capricorn, "Free Fall," in March 1977 and followed it quickly with a second, "What If," which produced the hit single "Taking It Off the Top" and brought the invitation for them to star on the closing night of the Montreux International Jazz Festival in Switzerland on July 23, 1978. Immediately thereafter Capricorn released a double live album "Hotels, Motels and Road Shows" featuring the Dregs.

T. Lavitz succeeded Davidowski as keyboardist, and the band enjoyed great popularity on the nightclub and concert circuits and recorded a fourth and its most successful album, "Dregs of the Earth," for Arista in 1980. It was nominated for a Grammy as Best Instrumental Group in 1981.

ROY DRUSKY

Roy Frank Drusky's boyhood dream was to be a professional baseball player and he once had a tryout with the Cleveland Indians. But he soon realized that writing and singing songs was what he really wanted to do. He proceeded to put more than fifty on the charts between 1953 and 1977, including ten No. 1 records. He also went on to establish himself as one of the most popular stars of the Grand Ole Opry and is a director of the Opry Trust Fund.

Born June 22, 1930, in Atlanta, Drusky taught himself to pick a pawn-shop guitar while serving in the Navy. After service, he played in clubs and worked as a disc jockey for a Decatur radio station and then worked at Channel 11 television in Atlanta. He moved to Minneapolis as a deejay and club performer and recorded his first hit "Such a Fool" for Starday Records in 1953. This initial success led to contracts with Columbia and Decca. His composition "Alone With You" was a hit for Faron Young. He joined the Opry in 1958.

He made the Top Ten in 1960 with "Another" and repeated the performance in 1961 with co-written releases of "I Went Out of My Way" and "I'd Rather Loan You Out." In 1963 he had a hit with "Second Hand Rose." His first No. 1 record was a duet in 1965 with Priscilla Mitchell, "Yes, Mr. Peters." He was again in the upper charts in 1966 with "White Lightning Express" and "World is Round." He had three singles in the charts in 1967 and in the 70's scored with "All My Hard Times," "Close to Home," and "Betty's Song."

Other Number One hits include "Three Hearts in A Tangle," "Long, Long Texas Road," "Jody and the Kid," and "Strangers."

He's done country music movies, toured extensively at home and abroad, issued more than thirty-five albums, won more than two dozen music awards and established his own music publishing firm, Funny Farm Music.

A devout layman in the Seventh Day Adventist Church, he

stopped doing "drinking and cheating" songs, including his greatest hit, "Yes, Mr. Peters." He and his wife Bobbye and their three sons live on a farm near Nashville.

Roy Drusky

WALLY FOWLER

The name of Wally Fowler, who was born near Rome, Georgia, and grew up singing in a little country church in Bartow County, is not a household word; but those of some of the superstars he helped get their starts are, and any aficionado of gospel music can tell you that he is the father of the "All Night Gospel Sings" which have been packing auditoriums throughout the southeast and much of the remaining eastern half of the United States since the 1950's.

A list of his firsts in the entertainment business is mind-boggling. He took on a young guitar picker by the name of Chet Atkins as his co-host on his Midday Merry-Go-Round program on radio station WNOX in Knoxville, Tennessee for nine months in 1944 and 1945. He was the founder and original baritone for the Oak Ridge Quartet, now known as the fabulously successful Oak Ridge Boys, and worked with them on the "Prince Albert" portion of the Grand Ole Opry from 1946 through 1950. He introduced Hank Williams to general manager Hank Stone of the Grand Ole Opry. He founded Bullet Records and produced Francis Craig's smash hit "Near You." He wrote Eddy Arnold's first million-selling song, "That's How Much I Love You;" the gospel classic "Wasted Years," which has been recorded by 56 gospel groups and individuals and which Elvis Presley was scheduled to revive at the time of his death; and, with Warren Roberts, "May The Lord Bless You Real Good," which was Dean Martin's hit song from his movie "Ada." He gave the late Patsy Cline her first professional singing job on a program he produced in Virginia in the early 1950's and he arranged Elvis' first audition with the Blackwood Quartet which was where Elvis demonstrated for the first time how he could make women in an audience go wild. (His continuing friendship with Presley culminated in his writing two songs, "A New Star in Heaven" and "He's Never Alone," which are featured on his album "Wally Fowler Sings a Tribute to Elvis Presley," along with his recorded recollections of his first meeting with Elvis. The album has been described as the "one sincere Elvis tribute.")

Although the first singing group he formed, "The Georgia Clodhoppers," specialized in bluegrass music, Fowler's first and greatest love is gospel singing, and it is in that field that his name is best known. He sang with the legendary V. O. Stamps over Station KRLD in Dallas, Texas, before staging the first of his "All Night Gospel Sing" concerts in 1946 at the Ryman Auditorium in Nashville. It packed the 3,400 maximum seating capacity of that hall and started Fowler on a 17-year career of producing such concerts monthly in the major southeastern cities of Atlanta, Memphis, Birmingham and Nashville and later into the major centers of the north, midwest and southwest. His shows consistently proved they could outdraw any other kind of entertainment, including wrestling and circuses, and were the subject of a number of national magazine articles, including one done by Furman Bisher for The Saturday Evening Post entitled "They Put Rhythm in Religion." Fowler also engaged in litigation with his brother and sister-in-law over his rights to the name "The Original Wally Fowler Gospel and Spiritual All-Night Singing Concert."

Fowler, who is now 75, went on to realize his lifelong ambition of having his own recording label with the establishment of his Dove Records International, Inc., which specializes in the recording and publication of gospel music, his own and others.

JESSE FULLER

Jesse Fuller never knew the exact date of his birth in 1896 in Jonesboro, Georgia, because he was "given away" by his mother. But he had music in his soul which began coming out when he made his own mouth bow and guitar at the age of seven while living near Macedonia, Georgia, and persisted through many menial jobs ranging from working in a Brunswick, Georgia, chair factory to stretching canvas for a circus.

It culminated in his becoming an acclaimed folk-blues artist in California who invented a unique instrument he called a "fotdella." He wrote "San Francisco Bay Blues" made popular when recorded by Peter, Paul and Mary and performed at numerous folk festivals and with such legendary rock groups as the Rolling Stones and the Animals before he died in Oakland in 1976.

Fuller was "discovered" shining shoes near the gate of United Artists by Douglas Fairbanks Sr., who got him bit parts in several movies, but he forsook Hollywood for Oakland where he worked in construction by day and came to the attention of jazz and folk artists in San Francisco through his musical dates at night. He opened another shoeshine stand which became a hang-out for folk music fans in Berkeley and became a close friend of folk-singer Barbara Dane with whom he performed. He also invented his "fotdella" which was a one-man band rig featuring piano strings and cymbals or washboard played by right and left foot pedals respectively, harmonica and kazoo held by harness and six or twelve string guitars. He was the uninvited hit of the 1959 Monterey Jazz Festival which publicly brought him invitations to similar festivals throughout the United States and to England in 1966 to star with the Stones and the Animals.

Although it was written in 1954, "San Francisco Bay Blues" did not become known until it was recorded by Peter, Paul and Mary. It then kindled an interest in Fuller's music that resulted in nine albums of his work being issued between 1958 and 1967 by

92

Prestige, GT, Arhoolie and Fantasy Records, of which only the latter's "Brother Lowdown" remains commercially available.

Despite all the hardship and heartache of his life, Fuller never became bitter or despairing and his music was always upbeat and featured messages of hope and beauty.

TERRI GIBBS

When success happened for Terri Gibbs, the blind country soul singer from Grovetown, Georgia, whose smokey, bluesy, velvet-throated voice has been described as the deepest alto in music, it came with the impact of the opening of the flood gates of a high dam. But in perspective it was far less the Cinderella story it has been called than the culmination of years of stubborn dreaming and struggling dues-paying of which the miracle is that it happened at all.

Not even Jimmy the Greek would quote odds on a country artist's first single being released on a major label, becoming a Top Ten smash, achieving crossover success, putting her on the Grand Ole Opry and winning for her more than a dozen of the industry's top nominations and awards. But that's the way it was with Terri's "Somebody's Knockin'" in 1981.

It all seemed like a lot of magic except to those who knew the years of study, practice, hard work and effort; and the disappointment, persistence, hope and plain luck which made it more than just the aspirations of a girl born sightless on June 15, 1954, who could play tunes she heard on the piano from the age of three.

Terri's unique singing and playing style which evokes surprise from initial listeners that she is a white woman developed from a childhood of playing the piano instead of playing with dolls. She listened to a mix, from the harmonies of the Everly Brothers, to Loretta Lynn, Patti Page and Pat Boone, from the soul of Aretha Franklin and Isaac Hayes to the rhythm and blues of Ray Charles to the rock of Elvis Presley and Janis Joplin. It is almost a shocking experience to see her for the first time rhythmically rocking on the piano bench in almost the same way as Ray Charles whom she never will see and singing with the same bluesy touch as he.

Gibbs' first public performances were of gospel songs in church and winning high school talent contests. At seventeen she opened an Augusta performance by Bill Anderson and at eighteen met

Chet Atkins who invited her to send him a tape and then helped her come to Nashville to do a demo which somehow got lost until it came to the attention of Nashville songwriter/producer Ed Penney five years later.

During the interim she played keyboard and sang back-up first for a local band called Sound Dimension and then formed her own group which performed to local acclaim at Augusta's Steak and Ale Restaurant, singing fifty songs in three sets nightly for five years.

When Penney found the tape, it did not have her address; but luckily, one of the many other demos she subsequently made and sent to everyone in Nashville reached him shortly thereafter. Thus, the contact was made which resulted in her "Somebody's Knockin' " album and single of the same title being issued by MCA to almost instantaneous popularity.

In April of 1981 she received the Top New Female Vocalist Award of the Academy of Country Music. In June she was nominated Most Promising Female Artist of the Year by Music City News. Record World Magazine named her Most Promising Female Vocalist of Adult Contemporary Music and ranked her third as Top New Female Vocalist in Pop Music and in the ten Top Adult Contemporary Female Vocalists and in October gave her its Top New Female Vocalist of the Year in Country Music Award. In September the Atlanta Songwriters Association gave her the Georgia Recording Artist of the Year Awards which was followed shortly by an invitation to appear on the Grand Ole Opry. In October the Country Music Association nominated her for Female Vocalist and Single of the Year and presented her with its New Horizon Award as the top new talent of the year. That same month Cash Box Magazine named her New Female Vocalist of the Year in Country Music and she was presented the Grammy Award for New Female Vocalist in Los Angeles.

She followed her inital success with a second album, "I'm A Lady," from which singles were issued both of the title song and the old Tony Bennett hit, "I Wanna Be Around." Single releases also were made of "Rich Man" from her first album and of "Wishing Well" which was written by David Hensley and herself. She since has formed her own music publishing company, changed the emphasis on her career from concerts to music writing and purchased a white antebellum home in Augusta where she lives and works with her pet chickens which are named after her favorite singers.

Terri attributes her success to her independence and stubbornness and not having been petted and pampered because of her blindness. She does not like "to think I can't do something" and says, "If somebody tells me I can't do something, I'll kill myself to do it."

Terri Gibbs

VERN GOSDIN

It was a supreme bit of irony that it was a song entitled "Yesterday's Gone" that made a 40-year-old dream to sing on the Grand Ole Opry come true for Vern Gosdin after he had all but given up on the ambition to pursue a glass and mirror business in Atlanta.

Born August 5, 1934, in Woodland, Alabama, Vern and his brother, Rex, who lived at Hampton, Georgia, listened to the Opry on a battery radio on the family farm and dreamed of growing up to sing like the Louvin Brothers. In the early Fifties they had their Gosdin Family Gospel Show on Birmingham Station WVOK, but Vern left to come to Atlanta to support himself by selling ice cream while seeking work as a country artist.

In 1956 he went to Chicago to run a country music nightclub and in 1960 joined Rex in California in a bluegrass group, the Golden State Boys. He later switched to a group called the Hillmen whose leaders, Chris Hillman, and Clarence White recorded a song written by Vern, "Someone to Turn to," for the soundtrack of the movie "Easy Rider." He and Rex did "Hangin' On" for the Bakersfield International label, and it rose to eighteen on the charts and brought them a contract with Capitol in 1967 for which they recorded "Till the End," by Vern's wife, Cathy. However, divorce and disillusionment with the lack or progress on their career brought a breakup of the act, and Vern returned to Atlanta to open his business.

In 1976 producer Gary Paxton, whom Vern had known in Los Angeles, called and asked if he would be interested in re-issuing "Hangin' On." Consequently, he went to Nashville, where he did "Yesterday's Gone" with Emmylou Harris singing the harmony instead. That song made the Top Twenty and resulted in an album which resurected "Till the End"; this recording made it to the Top Five.

This publicity brought an invitation to the Opry and a succession of hits beginning with "Mother Country Music" in October 1977 and continuing with "It Started All Over Again" and "Break My Mind" in 1978. Early that year he and Rex got back together to record "Never My Love," which was a hit, and they resumed performing together for concert dates. In 1979 he charted with "You've Got Somebody, I've Got Somebody" and "Sarah's Eyes"; he followed with the hit "Too Long Gone," in 1981, and he began 1983 with the Top Ten success of his own composition "If You're Going To Do Me Wrong (Do It Right)."

He had his first Number One Song in 1984 with "I Can Tell by the Way You Dance" in Compleat Records.

Vern has since turned his business over to his sons and has a successful full-time career as a performing vocalist, guitarist, mandolinist, banjo player and songwriter.

Rex Gosdin, one of Georgia's most talented songwriters and artists, died in 1983.

Vern Gosdin

JACK GREENE

Whatever future success he may achieve, Jack Greene, who got his musical start in Atlanta, will have to go some to top the year 1967. His recording of Dallas Fraizer's "There Goes My Everything" won him Country Music Association Awards for Song, Single, Album, and Male Vocalist of the year, a Grammy nomination, top awards of Billboard, Cash Box and Record World magazines and Music City News and an invitation to join the Grand Ole Opry.

Born January 7, 1930, in Maryville, Tennessee, Greene started on the guitar when he was eight and came to Atlanta in the late 1940's to play guitar with the Cherokee Trio and guitar and drums with the Rhythm Ranch Boys. He did a stint in the army and in 1953 joined the Peachtree Cowboys on WSB-TV.

Ernest Tubb noticed his talents and Greene joined Tubb's "Troubadours" in 1962. His versatility as a drummer, guitarist, back-up and solo vocalist made him a valuable member.

His unprecedented smash of "Everything" in 1967 was followed by "All the Time" and a second Grammy nomination for it in 1968. He and Jeanie Seely also did a series of duets which brought them Grammy nominations. He parted company with MCA after several successful albums and signed with a new label, Frontline, and returned to the charts with such singles as "Rock I'm Leaning On" and "Devil's Den." His band was once called "Jolly Green Giants" but is now known as "The Renegades." He lives in Hendersonville, Tennessee.

Isaac Hayes

ISAAC HAYES

When Isaac Hayes was growing up in the mind-numbing poverty of a post-World War II cotton sharecropping farm north of Memphis, Tennessee, he blotted out the bitterness of his orphaned deprivation by making up songs in his head about birds and trees and indulging in his fantasies about growing up to be like his idols — Billy Eckstine and Nat "King" Cole.

But his wildest dreams never envisioned the actual realities of his music's winning an Oscar, his starring in the movies, his making it as the designer of fashion jeans and his residing in Atlanta's wealthiest neighborhood near the mansion housing the governor of Georgia.

Reaching those pinnacles require two cycles of rags to riches, but the rollercoaster progressions from youthful fieldhand to flamboyant performer to despairing bankrupt to respected professional never dimmed Hayes' basic goal in life to do all he could to fill the need of both black and white youths for "that positive impulse put to them in the hopes that it will deter them from doing negative things in life."

While establishing his shining bald head, outrageous wardrobes and luxurious cars as personal trademarks, he refused movie parts as pimps and drug dealers and devoted large amounts of his wealth to such worthy and largely unpublicized projects as building low-income housing projects and heading Atlanta's Empty Stocking Fund Drive.

Born August 20, 1943, near Covington, Tennessee, he was orphaned by the death of his mother and the desertion of his father before he was a year old and was reared by his sharecropping grandparents, who brought him up in the church and sought to instill in him the strength and determination to better himself. Because of field work his formal schooling was sporadic at best, and he recalls he soothed himself by sitting on the porch, making up songs, singing aimlessly to the sky and daydreaming about being like Cole and Eckstine. As he told Zoo World in a 1974 interview: "I used to sing about anything — the birds, the trees, work, cotton. It made me feel so good to close my eyes and be whatever I wanted to be. I knew someday, somehow I would get there." He sang in the church choir from the age of five and taught himself to play the church piano and organ by the time he was a teenager.

After moving to Memphis to pursue his musical dreams, he was working in a packing house when he got a job working one night a week as sideman for saxophonist Floyd Newman, a staff band member at Stax Records. Newman introduced young Isaac to its president, Jim Stewart, who auditioned and hired him in 1963 to take the place of Booker T, the staff pianist while he took leave to work on his college degree. Hayes began doing arranging, teamed with David Porter in writing and, with Porter and Booker T, became the nucleus of Stax' "Memphis Sound," backing Otis Redding on most of his recordings and working with Rufus and Carla Thomas.

Hayes' debut as a recording soloist came as the result of a drunken spree in 1967 during which he and a Stax vice president went to the studio and made a tape which, upon sober reflection, they thought good enough to be released as the LP "Presenting Isaac Hayes." It didn't make the charts, but it did lead to the 1969 album, "Hot Buttered Soul," which not only did it make the charts but also became No. 1 nationally and topped $2-million in sales by the end of 1970.

Isaac had his first hit singles in August 1969 with "Walk On By" and "By the Time I Get to Phoenix" and followed them with albums which placed him with the Beatles and Rolling Stones as performers who were platinum sellers. "Isaac Hayes Movement" was on the charts from mid 1970 until late summer 1971, "To Be Continued" during all of 1971, and "Black Moses" from late 1971 well into 1972; the sound track from the movie "Shaft" was a top challenger for Record of the Year in 1971. "In the Beginning" and "Live at the Sahara Tahoe" were album hits of 1972 and 1973, and his single hits of the period were "Our Day Will Come!" and "I Stand Accused" in 1970; "Never Can Say Goodbye," "Theme from Shaft," and "The Look of Love" in 1971; and "Do Your Thing," "Let's Stay Together," "Theme from 'The Man'," and "Ain't That Lovin' You" in 1972. His "Theme from Shaft" not only was No. 1 for both single and album in 1971 but also won Hayes the Oscar for the Best Song from a Motion Picture for that year.

The successes of the "Hot Buttered Soul" album and the "Walk on By" and "Phoenix" singles propelled him, reluctantly at first, into concerts, beginning with a gig in Detroit. He says he was "scared . . . butterflies from head to toe" until he got on and realized "my bald head really got them off," and from that point on he worked assiduously at developing the exotic image of his monkish appearance achieved through shaven head and dark glasses contrasting with glamorous costumes featuring multi-colored capes, leather shirts with fur cuffs, black tights and gold necklaces.

He also starred in the movies "Three Tough Guys" and "Truck Turner" and was a millionaire and owned mansions in Memphis and Beverly Hills before he was 30. But his extravagant lifestyle coupled with three marriages which produced nine children and philanthropies which sometimes got out of hand brought him to bankruptcy and near ruin in 1977.

He cut his losses, moved to Atlanta with his third wife, Mignon, and recouped his fortune by resuming his recording activities. He established the syndicated Top 20 radio show "Black Music Countdown" in 130 national markets, starred in the movie "Escape from New York," and designed, introduced and produced the Isaac Hayes Originals designer jeans and tops for men and women, featuring the "Isacki" top adapted from the kimono-like tunic worn by karate specialists of which he is one. He produced jazz albums with Donald Byrd and signed to star in and score films for H. I. S. Films International of Marietta, Georgia. After recouping his losses, he bought a mansion in Northwest Atlanta's wealthiest enclave not far from Georgia's Governor's Mansion. Here he devoted himself to charitable causes, ran ten miles a day and hoped to achieve his further ambition of appearing in a soap opera. Although his costumes are more subdued, his trademarks continue to be the shaven head accentuated by beard and dark glasses.

BERTIE HIGGINS

Like his great-great-grandfather, Johann Wolfgang von Goethe, Bertie Higgins is a crackerjack storyteller; but, unlike that illustrious ancestor, the Florida songwriter who now calls Atlanta home eschews the hellish for the romantic in choosing the themes for his tunes.

His smash hit "Key Largo," which marked him as one of the comers of the 80's, has an autobiographical premise no less schmaltzy than "boy meets girl, boy loses girl" interlaced with a lot of nostalgia about Bogart, Bacall and islands in the sun. And, as if in keeping with that classic premise of the movies of the 40's, the ultimate outcome of that song not only was to increase his fortune from the 25 cents he had in his jeans the day he and fellow Atlantan Sonny Limbo wrote it to more than a million dollars but also to complete the "boy gets girl" cycle with his subsequent marriage to his girlfriend Beverly Ann Seilberg, about whom it was written.

It is not that Higgins, who was born 38 years ago and christened "Elbert" in the picturesque Greek sponge-fishing village of Tarpon Springs on the Florida Gulf Coast, could not tell some devilish tales of his own rivaling those of Dr. Faust what with 18 years of poverty and his struggle in trying to get somone to listen to his songs. He is both intellectual and romantic and loves to tell stories which combine questions about life and the fantasies everyone dreams about living and loving in a tropical paradise. His love songs treat the efforts of mature males to understand and deal with the female psyche; his fantasy songs deal with the beauty and sensuality of the tropics; and his story songs combine past failings with future hopes all interwoven with the philosophy of "live it up today, for tomorrow we may die." Because he is first and foremost a storyteller, he currently is concentrating on his overriding ambition to be a successful screenwriter, and he already has sold a script, "Through the Eye," about dope smuggling on a shrimp boat to Twentieth Century Fox and is working on a script for a remake of "Key Largo."

All of the ingredients of Higgins' background and life are incongruous. Born of Portuguese, Irish and German extraction and reared in a Greek community, he at one time supported himself as a sponge diver and began his career in show business as a ventriloquist; he won top prizes both in talent contests for performing and at arts and crafts fairs for his self-designed, homemade dummies.

After acquiring a set of battered drums, he dropped out of St. Petersburg Junior College to join Tommy Roe's band, The Roemans, and played throughout the world with Tom Jones, the Beach Boys, the Rolling Stones and others, backing Roe on his greatest hits and playing with the Roemans on their own hit "Universal Soldiers." Tiring of travel, he returned to Florida to work at writing songs and to support himself by playing in nightclubs, but several recording deals fell through and the closest he came to success was the recording of his "Waiting for the Rain," which was successful for Emma Hanna in Australia and Patricia Dahlquist in Canada and the use of several of his original compositions by the ABC television program "20/20." During this period he also met and became a protege of actor Richard Boone, who tutored him in screenwriting.

He moved to Atlanta in 1980 and was sleeping in a bare apartment in Smyrna, Georgia, on a quilt given to him by his mother when he teamed up with Sonny Limbo, writer of Gladys Knight's superhit "Midnight Train to Georgia." He had a quarter in his pocket when he and Sonny — after spending a night drinking beer and watching the Humphrey Bogart-Lauren Bacall movie "Key Largo" on cable television — wrote a song by the same title based on Bertie's broken romance. Limbo persuaded his friend Scott McClellan of Pyramid Studios in Lookout Mountain, Tennessee, to record a demo of it. Atlanta music publisher Bill Lowery, who had known Higgins from his days with the Roemans, liked it and, with the addition of some more Bogart-Bacall touches which he suggested, sold it to Atlanta entertainment attorney Joel Katz and his new Atlanta-based label Kat Family Records.

Higgins and Limbo also wrote "Casablanca," "Down at the Blue Moon," "White Line," "The Tropics," "Port O' Call" and "Just Another Day in Paradise," the latter becoming the title of the album containing them all.

"Key Largo," promoted by a personal tour of radio stations in

105

the southeast by Higgins, was released in late 1981, was No. 1 in Atlanta by Christmas and by mid-1982 had reached No. 1 in Adult Contemporary, No. 8 in the Top 40 and the Top 50 in Country; and "Casablanca" simultaneously became a top hit in Japan. It not only made Higgins a lot of money but also earned for him the Atlanta Songwriters Association's Songwriter of the Year Award and a Proclamation of Commendation from Governor George Busbee.

In addition to working on his movie scripts in 1983, Higgins also toured with his band; issued a second album, "Pirates and Poets"; a single, "When You Fall in Love" expanded his efforts in the preservation of Florida wildlife, particularly the endangered pelican and made plans for the realization of his further dreams of establishing his own recording complex and Bertie Higgins' Key Largo Restaurant and Bar in Tarpon Springs.

Bertie Higgins

SHOT JACKSON

When the City of Nashville and the State of Tennessee joined in proclaiming October 16, 1980 as Shot Jackson Day, a plaque was presented to the virtuoso dobro performer and acclaimed guitar designer from Blackshear, Georgia. He was declared to be "The Pickers' Pick" to the accompaniment of a standing ovation from the Country Music Disc Jockeys of America.

With characteristic modesty the veteran picker suggested the accolade really should go to his long time friend, Roy Acuff, with whose Smokey Mountain Boys he played for many years and with whom he almost was killed in an automobile crash in 1965. But for those in attendance it was a richly-deserved tribute to a man who has had much to do with the development of country music through the design and manufacture of "The Sho-Bud," the world's most accepted steel guitar and the development of "The Sho-Bro" six-string, Spanish neck guitar, as well as in custom building and repairing the guitars of the biggest stars in the country music business.

"Aunt Irene" Robson is given credit by Shot for getting him started when she gave him his first guitar. He was fourteen and the instrument was a $2.98 special from Sears and Roebuck. He went on to become a regular on the Grand Ole Opry, having begun there almost forty years ago, and the undisputed King of the Dobro. He performed with the Bailes Brothers, Jonny and Jack, Kitty Wells and joined Acuff in 1956. He and his wife Darlene still perform some and he is featured in Hee Haw with the Clark Family.

He and Buddy Emmons started building steel guitars as a hobby and developed a business so successful that it now is a part of the musical instrument division of the Baldwin Piano and Organ Company. A modest man, Jackson returns to Pierce County, Georgia, often to do benefits and visit his sister, Hazel Conner. His mother, Mrs. Ruby Bowen Jackson of the Youmans Chapel Community, died about ten years ago. Shot recently underwent successful open heart surgery.

STONEWALL JACKSON

Yes, his real name is Stonewall Jackson and he really is a direct descendant of the revered Confederate general of that name. Yes, he is the only member of the Grand Ole Opry to be given a contract without first having a hit record to his credit. And yes, he writes most of his songs including the international hit "Waterloo" and more than 500 other titles.

Jackson is authentic country, born November 6, 1932 in North Carolina, and grew up in orphaned poverty on a pineywoods, sharecropping farm near Moultrie, Georgia. He was plowing a mule at eight and pulling a crosscut saw at ten. He traded an old bicycle for a cheap used guitar and taught himself to play. After a hitch in the Navy where he gained experience and confidence entertaining his shipmates he returned to Georgia. He worked two years on halves and cut pulpwood until he saved enough money to drive his dilapidated pickup to Nashville in 1956 to seek his fortune.

Luck smiled on him at his first stop, the studios of Acuff-Rose Publishing Company where he went to make some dubs of his songs. Wesley Rose himself heard them and set up an audition for him with George Hay, the "Solemn Old Judge" of the Grand Ole Opry who thought him "so country he's cute." After having to produce a birth certificate to prove his name was as real as his music, Jackson was sent on tour with Ernest Tubb who still calls him his son. He returned to be signed to a five-year contract with the Opry without having a single credit to his name. He has been an Opry regular ever since, saying it "makes you feel that you belong somewhere."

His Opry appearance brought him a recording contract with Columbia and his first release was "Don't Be Angry," which was one of the original dubs he did at Acuff-Rose. His first Top Ten hit was "Life to Go" which he wrote with George Jones under the agreement that the first to record it would give solo writing credit to the other. In 1959 his "Waterloo" took Jackson to the top of the pop as well as the country charts, and made him an international star. He was the most played artist on radio that year and made three appearances on American Banstand which further fueled his popularity.

In 1960 he scored with "Why I'm Walking;" in 1962 had two best-sellers in "A Wound Time Can't Erase" and "Leona"; in 1963 hit with "Old Showboat;" and in 1964 went to the top with the re-issue of "Angry" and the smash new "B.J. the D.J." Some of the many other hits over the years were "I Washed My Hands in Muddy Waters," "Stamp Out Loneliness," "Give It Back to the Indians" and "Promises and Hearts." All of his numerous albums have been top sellers and he has the reputation of never having cut a record which did not recoup its senior costs, a boast few of his contemporaries can make.

Now in semi-retirement, he devotes his time to his song publishing company, Tarp Tunes, named for his son who is drummer in his band, The Minutemen; working the Opry and playing five or six dates a month on the road. He lives the life of a "country farmer," which he remains at heart, on his "Lake Waterloo" near Brentwood, Tennessee.

Stonewall Jackson

ANDREW JENKINS

Blind Andy Jenkins was one of the first instant celebrities created by the electronic media. A product of the broadcast pioneering by Atlanta's Voice of the South, station WSB, he had a colorful career as a writer and singer of the instant "folk songs" he composed at the drop of a headline and as a radio evangelist with a national following from Mexico to Canada. Lambdin Kay, WSB's inventive manager, gave Jenkins not only his public exposure but also his non-existent title of "Doctor."

Andrew Jenkins was born November 26, 1885, at Jenkinsburg, Georgia, and died April 25, 1956, at Thomaston, Georgia. Like his contemporary, Riley Puckett, he lost his sight as an infant because of faulty medication. A self-ordained minister, he made his living selling newspapers in Atlanta. He had a fortunate second marriage with a widowed mother of three musical children, one of whom was Irene Spain, who was to become WSB's long-time staff pianist.

With Irene and her sister, Mary Lee, and brother, T. P., he formed the Jenkins Family, one of the first folk and gospel singing groups to sing on WSB after it went on the air in 1922 with a powerful signal which carried coast-to-coast. The group attracted such national popularity that they were signed to a recording contract with Okeh Records and made their first release in 1924 of two sides titled, "Church in the Wildwood" and "If I Could Hear My Mother Pray Again."

The group subsequently recorded under the varying names of Jenkins Family, Jenkins Sacred Singers, the Irene Spain Family, Blind Andy, Goodby Jenkins and Andrew Jenkins and Carson Robins.

Blind Andy got into "folk song" writing in 1925 when Okeh's Atlanta manager Polk Brockman asked him to do a song about the death of spelunker Floyd Collins in a cave in Kentucky. The result was "The Death of Floyd Collins," which he wrote in forty-five minutes. It became a minor success when done by

Fiddlin' John Carson and a major hit when recorded by Vernon Dalhart within two months of the tragic event. The Dalhart recording was backed in its second release by another Jenkins song, "The Dream of the Miner's Child," which stirred a never-fully-resolved copyright dispute with the writers of the almost identical English ballad, "Don't Go Down in the Mine, Dad."

Jenkins' success with the folk song approach inspired him to go on to do similar songs like "Billy the Kid" based on the Walter Noble Burns book, "The Wreck of the Royal Palm," based on the 1926 collision of the Southern Railway fliers, Ponce de Leon and the Royal Palm, near Rockmart, Georgia, and "The Tragedy on Daytona Beach" based on the 1929 death of race driver Lee Bible. Jenkins was very careful about registering his copyrights and, after his death, Irene was successful in pursuing royalties when Mahalia Jackson recorded his obscure "God Put a Rainbow in the Cloud," which she thought to be in the public domain.

Irene and Blind Andy also transcribed most of Fiddlin' John Carson's songs because neither he nor his daughter, Rosa Lee, could read music. One of Irene's later recollections was of her "Reverend" stepfather's requiring her to close the window before listening to some of Carson's mildly-suggestive lyrics which Jenkins referred to as "dirty words."

Jenkins' dim eyesight completely failed him in 1939, and although he knew Braille, Irene also did most of his paperwork. She recalled wistfully that had she known "Floyd Collins" was going to be such a big hit she would "have added a few grace notes to color its melodic simplicity" when she prepared the text-tune for Brockman.

Jenkins spent his final years preaching in Georgia revivals and engaging in radio evangelism on the powerful, uncontrolled radio stations across the Mexican border.

GLADYS KNIGHT
and
THE PIPS

The story that Gladys Knight was born singing instead of crying is apocryphal, but it certainly is true that her first memory is of standing on a chair at the age of four in 1948 to sing gospel songs before the congregation of the Mount Moriah Baptist Church in Atlanta and that, with the encouragement of her singing parents who had been members of the famed Wings Over Jordan Choir, her life since has been one musical success after another as the starring personality of the black singing and dancing rhythm and blues group Gladys Knight and the Pips, which has won three Grammys from seven nominations and has recorded five gold albums and eleven gold and two platinum singles, the latter two breaking all precedents by coming in the same year of 1973 on competing labels and both winning Grammys.

Gladys toured with the Morris Brown College choir before she was five, won the National Grand Prize on Ted Mack's Original Amateur Hour when she was seven and formed her first group at eight to sing at the birthday party for her brother Merald, who is known as Bubba. Besides herself, the group was composed of Bubba, their sister Brenda and their cousins Eleanor and William Guest; and their performance so impressed their uncle, James Wood, that he urged them to continue professionally. Then they took his nickname "Pip" as the group's name. Since that time the original quintet became a quartet when Brenda and Eleanor opted for marriage and families and the decision was made to go with an all-male back-up with the addition of another cousin, Edward Patton. Despite all the plays on the word and the jokes made about their name, the group never gave consideration to calling itself anything but "Pips"; Gladys explained that, in

112

addition to the deserved honor it pays a kinsman who helped them so much, they also like the definition of the word as "a seed" because "we're like a seed that goes into the making of a song."

The group began touring with Supersonic Attractions and its stars Sam Cooke and B. B. King and recorded its first single, "Whistle My Love" on the Brunswick label in 1958. It had its first hit in 1961 with "Every Beat of My Heart," which not only was both an R & B and pop success but also landed them in a court battle when three different labels issued it — Huntom of Atlanta, which made it a local hit and then sold its masters to V. J. Records, and Fury Records of New York, with which the Pips had signed a contract. Fury won the suit but not before the competing versions, one with an organ and the other with a piano background, registered No. 1 and No. 2 on the charts at the same time and eventually sold more than one million copies collectively. The publicity helped their second Fury release, "Letter Full of Tears," become an even bigger hit and assured the success of the album of the same title and the singles "Operator" and "You Broke Your Promise"; but the Pips were the ultimate losers because the company went bankrupt, and the group had several lean years while Gladys had a baby and the men had to struggle on their own in New York. They went to Max Records and scored with "Givin' Up Is Hard to Do" in both album and single releases; and, in 1966, over Gladys' objection, they signed with Motown which brought them not only new success but further litigation together with the anomaly of having platinum hits for both their old and new labels after they switched to Buddah Records upon expiration of the contract with Motown in 1973.

After minor hits with "Take Me in Your Arms and Love Me" and "Everybody Needs Love," they reached No. 2 with "I Heard It on the Grapevine" in 1967. This recognition brought them appearances on the Ed Sullivan Show, engagements at the Copa and other nightclubs and in Las Vegas and was followed with No. 15 "The End of Our Road" in 1968; No. 19 "The Nitty Gritty" and No. 17 "Friendship Train" in 1969; best-seller "You Need Love Like I Do" in 1970; and No. 7 "If I Were Your Woman" and Record of the Year nomination for "I Don't Want to Do Wrong" in 1971. They also charted with albums titled "Nitty Gritty," "Greatest Hits," "If I Were Your Woman" and "Standing Ovation." In 1972 the group had two single hits, "Help Me Make It Through the Night" and "Make Me the Woman You Come Home To" and 1973 the single "Daddy Could Swear, I

Declare" was a best seller for several months and three albums were big successes — "Neither One of Us" making the Top 10 Pop List, "Imagination" reaching the Top 40 and "All I Need Is Time" joining the charts.

It was 1973 that was their blockbuster year. Switching to Buddah, they released their greatest hit, "Midnight Train to Georgia," which sold more than 2,000,000 records and received a Grammy for Best R & B Vocal Performance. But Motown countered with a single they had done there before leaving, "Neither One of Us (Wants to Be the First to Say Goodbye)," which not only went platinum and earned a Grammy for Best Pop Vocal Performance but also was America's No. 1 song of the year. (The Pips, who left Motown because they objected to the Motown practice of having other artists cover their hits and because they felt that they were not being given the same kind of attention and help given Diana Ross and the Jackson Five, subsequently sued that label for royalties they claimed they never received for that final smash single.) They had a third million seller that year in "I've Got to Use My Imagination," which made them the biggest-selling recording group of 1973.

The roll continued in 1974: "I've Got to Use My Imagination" continued a four-week run through the Top 10; their new single "You're the Best Thing That Ever Happened to Me" reached No. 3; and their recording of Curtis Mayfield's "On and On" for the soundtrack of the movie "Claudine" gave them their fourth consecutive Gold Record for Buddah. In addition, the album "Imagination" brought Gladys an individual Grammy for Best Album by a Female Soul Artist. (The three Grammys Gladys and the Pips share from 1973-74 followed previous nominations in 1967 for "I Heard It Through the Grapevine," in 1969 for "Friendship Train," in 1971 for "If I Were Your Woman" and in 1972 for "Help Me Make It Through the Night.")

In 1975 Gladys and the Pips hosted a summer variety series for the NBC Television Network, and she starred in the movie "Pipe Dreams," for which the group also recorded the soundtrack. In 1978 they sued Buddah Records and its President, Art Kass, for $23 million because of unpaid royalties and the assignment of their contract without their consent to Arista Records. The litigation prevented them from recording for almost two years although they continued to perform together in concerts and nightclubs. The suit was settled in 1980. Then Columbia Records bought their contract, and Gladys and the Pips entered their third decade of performing with a new album titled "About Love" on that label.

All of the group make their homes in Atlanta. Gladys now has three children, two of them teen-agers, and when asked by Ebony Magazine to what she attributed the success of the group, she stated:

"One reason we've been able to stick together is because we pray before each show — pray for strength to stay humble, courage to keep pushing and the ability to reach people with our message."

Gladys Knight and the Pips

LEO KOTTKE

Leo Kottke, who was born in Athens, Georgia, September 11, 1945, is one of those rare musical geniuses from whom music is an end in itself. A self-taught virtuoso on the twelve-string guitar, he is ranked among performers on that instrument as one of the foremost in the world and one of the top two or three in the United States. But he has eschewed the fortune that talent could bring him through commercial concerts and recordings to play his own music on stages of his own choosing.

He learned to play the trombone in high school in Muskogee, Oklahoma and taught himself the flute, harmonica, violin and guitar. He concentrated on the guitar when he came under the influence of the folk music of Burl Ives, the Kingston Trio and Jimmie Rodgers and advanced to the music of Pete Seeger, Dan Reno and Red Smiley.

He left college in Minnesota to work in bars and coffee houses and in 1969 produced an album titled "12-String Blues" which attracted some attention. Takoma Records then produced a series of fairly-successful albums beginning in 1970 with "6-and 12 Sting Guitar" and continuing with "Mudlark" in 1971 and "Greenhouse" in 1973. Capitol Records put out his top-selling collection "Ice-Water," which sold 200,000 copies in 1974 and followed it the next year with "Dreams and Other Stuff." Chrysalis Records issued one titled "Leo Kottke" in 1977.

He received ovations on a concert tour of Europe, particularly in Germany in 1973, but since has chosen to live in relative obscurity in Minnesota and to perform to small audiences on his own terms.

116

BRENDA LEE

Brenda Lee has bridged more gaps than any other performer in modern musical history and has the records to show for it.

Although her most ardent fans continue to think of her in terms of "Little Miss Dynamite" who rocked her way to stardom through the medium of television in the mid-50's and 60's, she presently has the distinction of having sold more records than any other solo female singer in the world. These include hits across the spectrum from traditional country to hard rock and back to middle-of-the road pop.

She is credited with bringing national attention to Nashville as a pop recording center and is Music City's only true international star, having taped specifically for foreign markets in Japanese, Spanish, German, French and Italian. She draws even larger audiences abroad than she does in the United States, particularly in Japan where she holds the attendance record.

Brenda has sold more than 90 million records, including twelve Gold Records for singles sales of one million or more, over two dozen best-selling albums and twice that number of single chart successes.

By the time she was 21 she had over 32 successive chart records and, over the course of her career, has won every major music award except a Grammy for which she has had two nominations — for "Johnny One Time" in 1969 and "Tell Me What It's Like" in 1980.

Hers is truly a "rags-to-riches" story. Although she is now rich and famous, her childhood singing often was the difference between hunger and the family's having food on the table. This was especially true after her father was fatally injured in a construction accident when she was only eight. Her mother had to go to work in a cotton mill to support her and her brother and two sisters, all of whom Brenda subsequently put through college.

Born Brenda Mae Tarpley on December 11, 1944, in Lithonia, Georgia, she grew up in nearby Conyers, where she demonstrated

Brenda Lee

what her mother called "a God-given talent" as a toddler by repeating songs heard on the radio. At five she won a talent contest at the Conyers Elementary School Spring Festival by singing "Take Me Out to the Ball Game." That led to regular appearances first on "Starmakers Review," an Atlanta Saturday radio program, and then, before the age of seven on "TV Ranch," a production of Atlanta's WAGA-TV. She had to stand on a box to reach the microphone. Her first professional job was singing at a Shrine Club luncheon where she was paid twenty dollars.

In 1955, Peanut Faircloth, a disc jockey, offered her unpaid top billing on his television program and help in getting paid bookings in the area if her family would move to Augusta. He also persuaded Red Foley and his manager, Dub Albritten, to audition her. Foley immediately signed her on his monthly "Junior Jubilee" showcase for young talent which was televised by ABC-TV from Springfield, Missouri, in conjunction with his regular "Ozark Jubilee." Her popularity won her booking on the Perry Como Show, and she soon had appearances on the Steve Allen and Ed Sullivan Shows and guest star slots with Bob Hope, Red Skelton, Danny Thomas, Dinah Shore and others.

Albritten became her manager and, when she was eleven, arranged a recording contract with Decca Records. She then moved to Nashville, where she and producer Owen Bradley became friends and major figures in the development of the Nashville recording industry.

Her first record, Hank Williams' "Jambalaya," was cut on July 30, 1956. It was followed soon by "Dynamite," from which she got the tag which follows her today. She recorded her first Gold Record "Rockin' Around the Christmas Tree," in 1958.

Albritten launched her international career by booking her in Paris at the Olympic Music Hall in 1959 and created a worldwide sensation by touting her as "a 32-year-old midget" after the French promoter objected to signing a child. This was followed by successful engagements in Germany, Italy and England (where she later gave a command performance for the Royal Family); a month long tour of Brazil, where she was called "The Explosive Girl"; and engagements in Japan and Australia, where she was mobbed by screaming fans.

Her second million seller was Ronnie Self's "I'm Sorry," which created controversy because fourteen-year-old girls at that time did not sing grown-up songs about true love and heartbreak, but it bumped Chubby Checkers' "The Twist" from the top of the charts and established Brenda as a star who might be small in stature but one who had a big, bluesy voice which radiated emotion and stirred audiences.

She followed it with the hits "Eventually," "Anybody but Me," "Everybody Loves Me but You" and her third Gold Record "All Alone Am I." She cut a phenomenal 256 songs by the time she was twenty-one.

In April 1963, she married Ronald Shacklett, son of a Nashville contractor, when they were both eighteen and gave birth to the first of their two daughters one year later.

Brenda and Ronnie live in Nashville, and she now limits her work to six months a year, mostly in nightclubs at home and concerts abroad.

After her string of rock and pop best sellers, she returned to her country roots in 1972 and had an immediate success with Kris Kristofferson's "Nobody Wins." Her new sound, which brought her a second Grammy nomination after eleven years, is broader and more sophisticated than her usual style, but is regarded as a progression rather than a departure from the music for which she is famed.

Standing only 4′9″ tall, Brenda Lee probably is the tiniest of today's music stars, but only Johnny Cash, George Jones and Jerry Lee Lewis share her distinction of still producing country hits a quarter of a century after they first made the charts. All of them are nearly twenty years her senior, and every one of the current top female artists, from Loretta Lynn on down, are both older in age and younger in experience than Brenda.

Brenda Lee, Zell Miller, Freddy Weller and Razzy Bailey

MYLON LEFEVRE

Mylon LeFevre left his famed Georgia gospel-singing family in 1968 because he wanted "to dress differently and have longer sideburns" and to seek fame and fortune as a full-time rock 'n' roller.

Declaring he "didn't feel right about making money off God unless I was really living for Him," Mylon pulled up his family roots to record the solo album "We Believe," (featuring "gospel words with rock 'n' roll music") with Joe South and several future members of the Atlanta Rhythm Section. He went on to form his own band, Holy Smoke, and to take southern rock into New York long before the Allman Brothers and Lynyrd Skynyrd.

He spent four years doing 320 shows a year and trying to "get higher than anybody" with Jimi Hendrix and other musicians. In 1972 he and guitarist Alvin Lee went to England where they recorded the album "On the Road to Freedom" with Mick Fleetwood, Ron Wood and George Harrison as back-up session players. He returned to Atlanta in 1977 to sign a contract with Warner Brothers and do a comeback concert with the Atlanta Rhythm Section at the Fox Theater on New Year's Eve.

In 1979 he sought revival of his career in an album produced by hitmaker Allen Toussaint for the Mercury label appropriately titled "Rock and Roll Resurrection."

THE LEFEVRES

There may be individuals whose impact has been greater, but of all the groups that have had major roles in the development of modern gospel music in this country, none can claim to having made greater pioneering contributions to nor achieving more enduring popularity in the evolution that has brought gospel singing out of the Pentecostal churches and into the concert halls and recording studios of the nation than the LeFevres of Atlanta. Now into their 63 year and second generation of performing, the New LeFevres formed around the family of "Uncle Alf,' the youngest of the original LeFevres, are continuing to draw hand-clapping, foot-stomping audiences throughout the nation from the sons and daughter of the fans of their inimitable forebears.

The story of The LeFevres is one of musical talent, family love, religious faith and entrepreneural genius in equal parts which began in 1921 in Smithville, Tennessee, when the children of the musical LeFevre Family — Urias (lead), Alphus (tenor) and Maude (alto) — formed a trio to sing in churches and were so popular they continued together as a performing group to sing their way through Lee College in Cleveland, Tennessee. At the time, Alphus, the member with the "built-in smile," though only 12 years old already was a champion guitarist and fiddler and well on his way to achieving his goal of being able to play any instrument made.

One of their early concerts was in the Chattanooga church pastored by the father of Eva Mae Whittington, an eight-year-old musical prodigy whose long black hair came closer to reaching the pedals of the church piano than her feet, where 16-year-old Urias was smitten with love which grew into correspondence with and culminated in marriage to Eva Mae when she became 17. Eva Mae, who had begun singing at her father's street-corner services in McColl, South Carolina, at the age of five, was playing the organ by ear at six when she was so small she had to sit in her father's lap to reach the keys while he pumped the pedals

The LeFevres

and was studying classical piano at the age of eight, succeeded the second of the LeFevre sisters who left the trio for marriage and served not only as pianist and singer but also mistress of ceremonies. The group traveled with her father at first, but then hired a bass singer, reformed as the LeFevres and undertook a performing career that, with varying changes of personnel and locale and a few interruptions for reasons like illness and war, would continue with every-increasing success and popularity for the next 45 years.

In 1939 they moved to Atlanta and began holding concerts for which they charged admissions of ten cents for adults and five cents for children. They quickly attracted a following and in 1940 were signed by NuGrape and Orange Crush to do a regular radio show on WGST for $50 a week which drew more than 1,000 fan letters a day and continued for 10 years with interruptions for World War II service by Urias in the Navy and Alphus in the Army. Until they returned in 1943, Eva Mae sang with The Homeland Harmony Quartet; and upon their return, they began traveling throughout the South for weekend concerts while Urias worked with Georgia Power Company and Eva Mae worked in a dime store during the week. Although Eva Mae wanted to quit to become a full-time mother and housewife, Urias refused to continue without her — the wisdom of which decision was borne out by the popularity she achieved which culminated in her being twice named Queen of Gospel Music by the National Quartet Convention beginning in 1954 and to the Gospel Music Hall of Fame in 1978.

The first of Eva Mae and Urias' children, Pierce, was born in 1936 followed by Meurice in 1937, Andrea in 1939, Mylon in 1945 and several years later a retarded daughter, Monteia. In an effort to get medical help for Monteia, Eva Mae and Urias took church jobs in Philadelphia for two years and Eva Mae sold her furniture a piece at a time to pay for treatments. She ultimately had a nervous breakdown caring for and worrying about the child, but she recovered and the family moved back to Atlanta and The LeFevres went back to performing to achieve the height of their popularity in the 50's and 60's.

Urias proved an innovative manager. Under his direction, the group became the first to use more than one microphone, to use musical instruments other than the piano played by members as they sang, to wear red jackets on stage, to own and travel by custom tour bus and to build, own and operate their own recording studio. When the group was sidelined after a bus wreck in which Alphus suffered a broken leg, Eva Mae's children formed their own group called the LeFevreairs which went on the road with Pierce playing the trumpet, Meurice the trombone and all of them singing. They got good reviews, with Pierce being called "the Pat Boone of Gospel Singing" for his smooth baritone voice and later becoming a full-fledged member of the adult group.

During the 60's the group expanded to six and at times, with the addition of various of Eva Mae and Urias' children, numbered as many as nine. Several outsiders were incorporated from time to time and two of those alumni have gone on to achieve fame in their own right with their own groups — Hovie Lister with the Masters V and Rex Nelon with the Rex Nelon Singers.

With characteristic foresight, Urias established a television production company, "Programming, Inc.," in the early 60's which initiated the syndicated Gospel Singing Caravan which was shown nationwide featuring The LeFevres and four other groups and Eva Mae as MC. The rating of that program exceeded the combined ratings of Red Skelton and Gomer Pyle when played in prime time and made The LeFevres a household word throughout America and Eva Mae the foremost female gospel singer of the nation. Demands for public appearances and concerts grew and they drew record crowds at many fairs in the United States and Canada and drew overflow audiences to some of the largest auditoriums of the nation. At the height of their popularity, they were traveling more than 100,000 miles in more than 40 states each year, had a fan club with a list of more than 3,000 members and, in addition to the Caravan, were appearing in three weekly television shows in Atlanta, Augusta and Columbus and five radio programs in Georgia.

The LeFevres also founded The LeFevre-Sing Publishing Company, The LeFevre Sound Corporation and the "SING" record label. They distributed records nationally for several major groups and produced and distributed television programs for themselves, Bill Anderson, The Chuck Wagon Gang, The Rangers and other popular groups and performers of the period.

They stayed on top until Urias retired in the mid-70's and Eva Mae retired in 1977. Urias died of cancer in 1978 and Mylon left to pursue an individual career and enjoyed considerable rock success. But the family tradition is being continued by "Uncle Alf" who, at the age of 73, is heading up The New LeFevres featuring his daughter, Marla, and his son, Scott, who recently was named Best Bass Singer in a midwestern talent poll. Proving that "Uncle Alf" has not lost the touch is the fact that in 1982 he received the Favorite First Tenor Award in a poll taken by Gospel Music News. The New LeFevres complain that, although they have bridged the generation gap, they have a hard time keeping up with him.

Eva Mae continues to enjoy her status as head of the clan and, while she no longer performs with the group, she does sing in church and gives concerts of her own. But wherever she goes she still is hailed as the "First lady of Gospel Music" and, of her long, eventful and colorful singing career says:

"I sacrificed a lot to be a gospel singer. I never had a social life. I never got to spend a lot of time with my children. I feel I was anointed from my mother's womb to sing and preach the savlation of God. I gave up a lot to sing His praises and to tell of His love, but to me it was worth evey minute of it . . . If I had to do it all over again, I'd do it the same way. I am a gospel singer and I will be a gospel singer until I die."

LAWANDA LINDSEY

LaWanda Lindsey started singing on her father's country music radio station in Savannah, Georgia, and with his band, The Dixie Show Boys, in and around that coastal Georgia city when she was only five. But after her discovery at the age of 14 by Conway Twitty's business manager, she signed her first recording contract with Chart Records and moved to Nashville.

Her first record, "Beggars Can't Be Choosers," and all of her 37 singles released through 1975 charted in all three trade magazines and her duet "Wild Mountain Berries" with Kenny Vernon reached the highest levels.

When invited by Buck Owens to succeed Susan Raye as the featured singer with the Buckaroos, she moved to Bakersfield, California in the mid-70's and switched to recording for Capitol Records, which issued her hits with "Today Will Be the First Day of the Rest of My Life," "Sunshine Feeling," "Hello Trouble," "Hello Out There" and "I Ain't Hangin' Round."

Since 1975 the 30-year-old Georgian has concentrated on songwriting with one of her biggest successes being "Wave Bye Bye to the Man" recorded by Lynn Anderson.

The Lewis family

THE LEWIS FAMILY

When Roy Lewis, Sr., left his fundamentalist home when fiddling was regarded as "the devil's work" to get married in 1925, one of the first things he and his new bride, Pauline, did after setting up housekeeping in Lincolnton, Georgia, was to buy a banjo, fiddle, guitar and mandolin to go with the guitar she already owned. Although they did not realize it at the time, it was the beginning of a musical dynasty which in three generations would transform the Lewis Family into "America's First Family of Bluegrass-Gospel Music."

Since they began performing together in 1951 and became pioneer stars on the new medium of television in 1954, the Lewises have played to more than five million people throughout the nation, including standing room only audiences at Lincoln Center in New York and the Smithsonian Institution in Washington, D. C. They have recorded forty-one albums; they travel in a $175,000 bus for which they paid cash and are in great demand at folk music and bluegrass festivals and country music concerts.

Headed by the patriarch known as "Pop," the Lewis Family today is composed of him, daughters Miggie Lewis, Polly Williamson and Janice Phillips, sons Wallace and "Little Roy" and grandsons Travis and Lewis Phillips. The daughters sing the traditional three-part gospel harmony; Polly plays the piano; the grandsons play bass and banjo; Wallace takes care of the instrumental back-up; everybody sings and "Little Roy" is the star and the catalyst who holds the group together with his virtuoso Scruggs-style banjo picking and talent for comedy. Mother Pauline has given up singing and playing the guitar to handle the sale of albums and the other chores of business management.

Station WJBF-TV in Augusta, Georgia, invited the family to do a live weekly program shortly after it went on the air in 1954, and although the slot has changed from the prime time Tuesdays of the first ten years, they have not missed a week since and still enjoy tremendous ratings at 7:30 A.M. on Sundays with their

129

shows being taped and syndicated nationally. In addition, they are regulars on the nationally syndicated "Nashville R. F. D." and have been featured at the Grand Ole Opry. They record for Starday and Cannon labels.

"Little Roy" has become a successful recording single with his albums of banjo and acoustic guitar, the latest of which contains liner notes authored by the Statler Brothers, the Osborne Brothers and Chet Atkins, who has been a family booster since he first caught the syndicated show at his daughter's home in Memphis. Grandson Lewis Phillips, though only eleven, has been singing and playing the banjo since he was four years old; he made his network television debut with Dolly Parten and Carol Burnett on the CBS Special, "Carol and Dolly in Nashville," in 1979. His performances, like those of his uncle, never fail to bring down the house. Another early booster was Mrs. Mamie Eisenhower, who became a fan during her visits to Augusta with her husband when he was President.

Although their music is mostly traditional country gospel, the Lewis Family members do not preach or regard themselves as "psalm singers." While their most requested song is the gospel number "Just One Rose," their programs also include popular secular selections such as "Cripple Creek" and "Rocky Top." The critics regard their style as bluegrass and give the Lewises high marks for it; but "Pop," who is nearly eighty, still plays all the instruments and sings, says he "never knew he was playing bluegrass music until a fellow said he was. I thought all along we was playing Lewis Family music."

The secret for their appeal and success is said to be "the basic honesty of their powerful and uplifting music," which is all Roy and Pauline set out to make when they and their growing family first played for their own enjoyment and for audiences in rural churches in northeast Georgia and western South Carolina.

HOVIE LISTER

V. O. Stamps of Dallas, Texas, elevated gospel-singing from churches to concert halls with his Stamps-Baxter Quartets and song, "Give The World A Smile," but it was Hovie Lister, the handsome Baptist preacher from Greenville, South Carolina, who now lives in Atlanta, Georgia, whose sense of style and flair for showmanship gave this music form class and chic.

Believing fervently that "God didn't intend for religion to wear a long face," Lister made his Statesmen Quartet, formed in 1948, one of the most popular gospel groups in America, even to the point of winning the Arthur Godfrey Talent Scouts competition of network television, without crossing that thin line between religious and secular music like contemporaries such as the Oak Ridge Boys.

Furman Bisher wrote in an article for The Saturday Evening Post that Lister and the Statesmen "put rhythm into religion" and were in the forefront of the groups which made all-night gospel singing a post-World War II entertainment phenomenon which could outdraw symphony, jazz and ballet concerts, circuses, basketball tournaments and wrestling matches in most of America east of the Mississippi River and large portions of the country west of it. At the height of their popularity they traveled 100,000 miles a year throughout the nation in a custom-designed sleeping bus singing to an average of 2500, and upwards of 10,000 people per concert and once appearing before an aggregate of 60,000 over a five-day period during a revival in Detroit. They owned four Gospel Music Publishing Companies, operated recording and television production companies jointly with The Blackwood Brothers and produced their own syndicated television show, "Singin' Time In Dixie." They also recorded for RCA for which their version of "This Ole House" was a best seller.

Distinguished by his Clark Gable mustache, wavy hair and toothpaste smile, Hovie, in addition to his sharp promotional

Hovie Lister and the Statesman Quartet

instincts, is an accomplished pianist and singer, the grandson of a South Carolina music teacher who grew up playing for a family quartet, the Listers, from the age of 14. For a time he was featured with the famed LeFevres until he branched out on his own in the late 40's with Tenor Denver Crumpler, Lead Jake Hess, Bass Jim (Big Chief) Wetherington and Baritone Doy Ott as the Statesmen Quartet. Jack Toney later succeeded Hess and Roland "Rozie" Rozelle, acknowledged to be one of the greatest tenor voices in Gospel Music, replaced Crumpler. Lister was best know for his flamboyant piano style, but he also would switch places with Ott for some emotional, crowd-pleasing solos of his own. A succession of Georgia Governors designated them as Georgia's Official "Ambassadors of Good Will."

Lister is an ordained Baptist minister who, throughout his years of travels, always came back to fill his country-church pulpit at the little Mount Zion Baptist Church near Marietta, Georgia, from which he refused to take any salary, insisting the pastorate helped "keep my feet on the ground." He defends the modish dress and upbeat entertaining style of his groups vigorously: "If it takes shaking my hair down, beating a piano like Liberace or Piano Red to keep these young people out of beer joints and the rear seats of automobiles, I'll do it. The devil's got his kind of entertainment. We've got ours. They criticize me, say I'm too lively for religion, but I get results. That's what counts."

In recent years Lister was the moving force in the consolidation of the Statesmen and Blackwood groups into The Masters V which carry on in the Statesmen tradition and already have a Grammy to prove it. With Lister as Manager and pianist, the Masters V also feature Deep Bassist J. D. Sumner and James Blackwood along with former Statesmen Rozelle and Hess.

In 1984, after 40 years in the gospel music field, Lister was selected to the Gospel Music Association's Hall of Fame.

BILL LOWERY

If there is any one overriding fact in the larger-than-life success story of Big Bill Lowery, the entrepreneural genius who has made Atlanta one of the recognized recording capitals of the music world, it is that he thrives on proving that he can do what others predict cannot be done. He beat cancer when no company would insure him against it. He built Radio Station WQXI into the heavyweight contender which went head-to-head with the un-disputed champion of the Atlanta airways, WSB. He had the last laugh on the New York publishers who predicted he never would be a successful music publisher in Atlanta. He came back from the bankruptcy of one of his early companies with a musical conglomerate bearing his name that rose in eight years to become Broadcast Music's Number One Publisher in 1969.

No wonder that he is known by the title of "Mr. Atlanta Music" and was the first of many Georgia greats to be selected for inclusion in the Georgia Music Hall of Fame when it was created in 1979.

Perhaps the truest measure of Bill Lowery's contributions to the world of music would be to try to imagine the voids which would exist if he did not. There would never have been such hits as "Young Love," "Games People Play," "(I Never Promised You A) Rose Garden," "Walk On By," "Dizzy," "Walk A Mile In My Shoes," "Don't It Make You Wanta Go Home," "Sheila," "Be Young, Be Foolish, Be Happy," "So Into You," "Champagne Jam," "Down In The Boondocks," "Key Largo," "I Love The Nightlife," "Stormy," "Spooky," "Ahab The Arab," "Traces," "Be-Bop-A-Lula," "Misery Loves Company," "Reach Out Of The Darkness," "Moonlight Feels Right," "Imaginary Lover," "What Kind Of Fool Do You Think I Am," "Common Man," and many others among the more than 5,000 titles embracing every type of music in the catalogues of the Lowery Group of Music Publishing Companies which hold 20 Gold Records and have sold more than 75 million records since the original Lowery

Music Company, Inc., received its BMI license on October 1, 1952. Neither would there have been such artists and writers as Mac Davis, Ray Stevens, Brenda Lee, Joe South, Jerry Reed, Sonny James, Billy Joe Royal, Freddy Weller, Tommy Roe, Alicia Bridges, Susan Hutcheson, Frederick Knight, Bertie Higgins, Buddy Buie, J. R. Cobb, Robert Nix, Ray Whitley, Dennis Yost, the Classics IV, the Atlanta Rhythm Section, the Tams, Starbuck and a host of other stars and groups.

Bill Lowery was born in the bayou country of Leesville, Louisiana, studied radio dramatics in California at Taft California Junior College under Raleigh Borrell of the Pasadena Playhouse and, after radio-announcing stints in Shreveport, Louisiana; Hot Springs, Arkansas; Oklahoma City, Oklahoma; and Wichita Falls, Texas; became the youngest radio station manager in the nation when hired at the age of 21 to direct the construction and programming of Radio Station WBEJ in Elizabethton, Tennessee.

A trip to Atlanta to attend the Georgia Tech-Alabama Football Game in 1946 brought him to the decision to ask his employer to seek a radio station permit in Atlanta and thus in 1946 was born out of his inventive mind the name, news direction and programming format of Station WQXI which made "Qxie" a household word in Atlanta with its WQX "Eye Witness News" and its pop music programming which stole the Sunday morning listening audience and put the city's dominant station, WSB, into a ratings race from which it never has recovered.

Two years later he accepted an offer to go with Station WGST as a deejay, commentator and play-by-play broadcaster of Georgia Tech football games. He did three imaginative and popular weekday radio shows; "Mama Goes A Shopping," "Musical Tune," and "Who's Singing," but it was his Saturday morning "Uncle Ebenezer Brown" Show on which he played a country dialect character that propelled him into the recording/publishing business. As "Uncle Eb" he found himself being called about local talent and referring potential recording talent to record company executives. It was thusly that he discovered the songwriting genius, Joe South, who at the age of 12 walked into the studios at 6 A.M. one Saturday morning and talked his way onto the air.

He was stricken by cancer in 1951 and, in addition to the less-than-favorable prognosis of his doctors, was unable to get insurance on himself or to buy any annuities for the protection of his family. He voted not only to beat the disease but also to make himself and his family financially secure and followed up on the suggestion of Ken Nelson of Capitol Records that the music publishing business offered the best hope of providing his family with security.

One of the first people to contact him after he established the first of the companies now comprising The Lowery Group was Songwriter Cotton Carrier who, in 1953, brought him a gospel tune he had written, "I Have But One Goal," which Lowery himself recorded with the Smith Brothers, Smitty and Tennessee. It became an immediate hit and gospel classic, selling more than 150,000 copies. That marked the beginning of his association with Carrier who remains with him today as General Professional Manager of the Group. It also marked the beginning of attempts of New York music publishers to lure Lowery to that city, Hal Fein of Roosevelt Music telling him that "you'll never become a publisher in Atlanta or make phonograph records there."

Fein had to eat those words in less than three years when Lowery recieved the BMI Award in 1956 for his first million seller, "Be-Bop-A-Lula," the rock 'n' roll classic done by Gene Vincent. The next year he published the biggest seller in the history of Lowery Music Company, "Young Love," which not only was a simultaneous No. 1 record for both Sonny James and Tab Hunter on the country and pop charts that year but also was revived to become an international No. 1 best seller by Donny Osmond in 1973. It is a song which has been recorded by literally hundreds of performers the world over and marked the beginning of a succession of Lowery hits which has continued like waves on a beach since.

Working relentlessly to realize his dream to make Atlanta "THE music capital of the world," Lowery encountered his only failure in 1961 when his National Recording Corporation (NRC) folded not because of any failing on his part, but because of its inability to collect its money from its distributors. Starting over, he recouped and scaled new heights in the industry with platinum albums in the United States and Canada for The Atlanta Rhythm Section's "A Rock And Roll Alternative" and "Champagne Jam" and in 1969 winning two Grammys for Joe South's "Games People Play" as Song of the Year and Best Contemporary Song (it also winning a third Grammy for King Curtis as the Best

Rhythm and Blues Instrumental Performance). His "(I Never Promised You A) Rose Garden," the Joe South song which was a hit for Lynn Anderson, was BMI's Most Performed Song of the Year in 1971 and he received certifications for more than 2 million broadcast performances not only for it but also for "Young Love" and "Traces" and 1 million performances for "Games People Play," "Stormy," "Walk On By," and "So Into You."

The Lowery Group, in addition to Bill's publishing companies, also built along with Bob Richardson Atlanta's first state-of-the-art recording studio, Master Sound, and with Buddy Buie, the famed Studio One in Doraville, Bill Lowery Talent which booked the Group's artists throughout the world and managed many of the artists such as Ray Stevens, Tommy Roe, Billy Joe Royal, Joe South, etc. In 1969 BILLBOARD MAGAZINE rated the group as the second largest music publishing house in the nation based on record chart activity, reporting it to be a $5-million annual operation. Today Lowery has only one recording facility—the just recently completed Southern Tracks Studio, one of the most modern studios in the South, built and dedicated to the Vice President of The Lowery Group, Mary Tallent, who was killed in an auto accident in 1983.

In recognition of his leadership in the industry, Bill has served twice as National President of the National Academy of Recording Arts and Sciences, is a member of the Boards of Directors of the National Music Publishers Association and the Country Music Association, is Past President of the Country Music Hall of Fame and serves on the NARAS Hall of Fame Elections Committee. The Bill Lowery Scholarship Fund was established in his honor at Georgia State University's School of Commercial Music in Atlanta in 1977 and in 1979 he was the first inductee upon the creation of the Georgia Music Hall of Fame. He has taken a leadership role in the yearly observance of Georgia Music Week under the sponsorship of the Music Industry Committee of the Georgia Senate and is a principal exponent of the establishment of a Georgia Recording Commission patterned after the highly-successful Georgia Film Commission.

A rotund man of physical proportions equal to his reputation and achievements, Lowery, with his flowing mane of silver hair, takes delight in being described as "Santa Claus without a beard," and sets great store by his reputation for being "the type individual that knows no defeat and is always certain that anything can be accomplished."

Bill Lowery

ROBERT MCDUFFIE

When the world-renowned violin virtuoso Yehuti Menuhen needs a chair partner for a sextet these days, he passes over his illustrious contemporaries for a brilliant young Georgian, 25 year-old Robert McDuffie of Macon, who is being heralded by the critics as the most promising of the rising new school of young American violinists. But if Bobbie McDuffie had his druthers, he would rather be playing "The Star Spangled Banner" at the beginning of one of the games of the Atlanta Braves of which he is a self-pronounced "fanatic."

Although a late bloomer by the standards of Menuhen who made his debut at the age of seven, McDuffie's performance at the Metropolitan Museum in New York in December 1983 was reported by The New York Times as "so polished and poised ..." that there was almost a sense of nonchalance, and The Washington Post called him a player "with power and abandonment." Whatever the adjective it is unanimously conceded that he is on the road to being the foremost among the first generation of a new musical movement which is shifting the strongest and most talented violinists from Europe and Russia to the United States.

Since leaving Macon at the age of 16 to study under the acclaimed Dorothy DeLay at the Julliard School of Music in New York City, McDuffie has amassed a record of credits which would be impressive for a performer twice his age.

At 19 he was guest soloist with the New York Pro Arts Chamber Orchestra on a tour of the Soviet Union and was invited back three years later as an individual to solo with major Russian orchestras.

He was guest soloist with the American Symphony Orchestra on its recent tour of Greece, toured the United States with the Danish Symphony and Czech Philaharmonic Orchestras and has performed with the Chicago, St. Louis and Baltimore Symphonies and at the Ravinia Music Festival.

He played with Menuhen, President of the Royal Philaharmonic Orchestra, at Carnegie Hall and was invited by him to England to be a sextet chair partner in March 1983 and back again for a similar performance with him in the Great Performers Series in February 1984.

Contemporary American Composer David Diamond has written a violin sonata for and dedicated it to him and arranged for him to perform Samuel Barbre's Violin Concerto in a private presentation for that terminally-ill composer.

Renowned Violin Teacher Jens Ellerman of the Cincinnati Conservatory of Music gave him a 225-year-old Gagliano violin.

Leonard Bernstein has adopted him as a protege and consults with and advises him about his work and career often.

U. S. Supreme Court Justice Harry Blackmun invited him to perform at a party for Justices of the Supreme Court and their guests and has become one of his foremost patrons and friends.

He has been named Summer Artist-in-Residence at the Apsen Music Festival in Colorado where he schedules rehearsals around watching Braves games on cable TV.

Since in classical music the road to success is the exact opposite to that in country music where the would-be star first strives to make a hit record and then tour, McDuffie presently is in the tour phase of his career in the hope of developing the stature and demand which will result in lucrative recording contracts. He spends only about 12 weeks a year in his small, austere one-bedroom apartment on Broadway in New York City to pay the rent on which he once accompanied a belly dancer at a party in New Jersey. The remainder of the time he plays with symphony orchestras and in concerts at factories and airports as part of the Affiliate Artists Program. He competed in the Naumburg International Violin Competition in 1981 which he lost because of a "memory slip" but brought him a coveted invitation to play with the Chicago Symphony considered to be America's best orchestra at the Ravina Music Festival.

The son and brother of gifted keyboard artists in Macon, McDuffie flunked piano and started playing the violin at the age of six, becoming a local celebrity performing for civic clubs and churches in the Macon area. However, in his early teen years he was much more interested in playing baseball and once was caught using a tape recording of himself to try to fool his mother into thinking he was practicing while he actually was on the

140

ballfield. Believing that he had exceptional talent if only given the proper instruction and opportunity, Mrs. McDuffie took him out of school and placed him in the hands of Mrs. Lay in whose home he lived until his graduation from Julliard.

It was there, McDuffie relates, that he developed the discipline to practice four hours a day and, as he put it, "where I got 'the fingers.' "

Described by Music Critic Larry Fennelly "as regular a guy as you could meet this side of the Athens KA House" and as one who "has the quiet confidence of those who are good at what they do but haven't let it disturb their composure or swell their head," McDuffie is modest and self-effacing in discussing his success, talent and technique. His style has been described as "intense and dramatic," but he emphatically denies that he is "hot-dogging" when he holds out his right foot and shakes his head while playing emotional passages. He prefers 20th Century music to Tchaikovsky and Mendelssohn and tries to give even the old masters what he calls "a fresh approach."

CLAYTON "PAPPY" MCMICHEN

Clayton "Pappy" McMichen was a great fiddler with an ego to match, and his success in infusing jazz, dixieland and other progressive techniques into traditional rural music made him a pioneer "crossover" artist who was a major figure in the development of country and western music in its popular present-day forms.

While he was clearly a leader in the establishment of musical trend, won numerous championships with his fiddling virtuosity, and could claim considerable credit in the development of the careers of such stars as Jimmie Rodgers, Merle Travis and Gene Autry, his own somewhat erratic course and sometimes abrasive personality cost him true stardom of his own.

Born into the third generation of a musical Scotch-Irish family, on January 26, 1900 in Allatoona, Georgia, McMichen learned to play the fiddle at the age of eleven from his uncles and father, who played Viennese waltzes for formal balls as well as reels for square dances. He moved to Atlanta to work as an automobile mechanic and to form bands. They were known as the Hometown Boys' String Band and the Lick the Skillet Band. He followed within days the appearance of Fiddlin' John Carson on radio station WSB in 1922, but later claimed that he predated Carson's performance by broadcasting earlier over Georgia Railroad's station which programmed privately for the entertainment of the passengers of its trains.

That same year he dethroned Carson as Georgia's Fiddlin' Champion and in 1926 was chosen by Gid Tanner to be lead fiddler for the Skillet Lickers band which he formed to record on Columbia Records and which quickly became the most popular string band in America. Throughout that relationship McMichen was to prove himself as difficult to get along with as his music was beautiful. He was constantly in friction with his fellow performers about personal credit and musical style. He was always wanting to experiment with new forms of what he called "modern music," particularly jazz, and to incorporate progressive treatments into their arrangements. From time to time he would form bands of his own to try his new approaches, one of which was known as McMichen's Mellow Men.

He considered Tanner's musical talents meager and insisted that he record off mike; consequently, Tanner was often inaudible. Although he conceded that it was the sweet tenor voice of Blind Puckett, a member of his first band, that sold The Skillet Lickers' records, he demanded the addition of his name to that of Puckett's on the labels of the band's recordings on the contention that the band's name was taken from that of his original group. He promoted Jimmie Rodgers to Okeh Records when Columbia Records, to which he and the Skillet Lickers were under contract, declined to sign him in competition with Puckett. He got into a number of disputes over songs he claimed to have written and was denied a copyright on "Bile Them Cabbage Down," which was declared to be in the public domain after he claimed to be its author.

He was a musical pioneer. Perhaps his greatest musical innovation was the development of the multiple-fiddling technique which was employed by the Skillet Lickers and which was the forerunner of western swing, an idea he said came from the symphonic orchestra he admired. He wanted to play popular songs on country strings rather than city horns and was the first to employ a clarinet in a country band; he composed and arranged music that he called "hot" country or "country" jazz.

When the Depression caused the Skillet Lickers to break up, he formed his Georgia Wildcats, which from their base in Covington, Kentucky, played McMichen's brand of country jazz with a Dixieland beat to record houses and on major radio stations around the country.

He played fiddle for Jimmie Rodgers on his first and many other records, and Rodgers made a hit of Pappy's "When It's Peach Picking Time in Georgia." Pappy discovered Merle Travis, a seventeen-year-old in the coal-mining town of Drakesboro, Kentucky, and let him make his first recording with the Wildcats. He helped Red Foley get his first job and got Gene Autry and his band signed at radio station WHAS in Louisville, Kentucky, from which Gene left to make his first movie. Pappy

143

worked as a disc jockey before retiring in 1954 and came out of retirement briefly to appear as the star of the Newport Folk Festival in 1964.

Pappy was for many years recognized as the Fiddling Champion of the United States, having won his first title in 1926 and his last in 1952. He died at the age of sixty-nine in Battletown, Kentucky, on January 3, 1970.

Clayton "Pappy" McMichen
Courtesy of the Country Music Foundation Library and Media Center

JAMES MELTON

The range of Georgia's handsome, personable tenor James Melton of Moultrie embraced the total musical spectrum; and because he was equally adept at singing folk songs like "Shortenin' Bread" in dialect and performing demanding operatic roles like those of Tamino in "The Magic Flute" or Ottavio in "Don Giovanni," he was said by United Press International at the time of his death at the age of 57 in 1961 to be "one of the most popular music personalities ever produced by the United States."

He not only was one of the most highly acclaimed singers of the Metropolitan Opera for a decade but also was perhaps even better known to the American public as a multi-media star of movies, radio and television whose career spanned more than 30 years.

A graduate of The University of Georgia, where he was a classmate of the colorful Bill Tate, and a performer in the summer operas produced by Hugh Hodgson, Melton went to New York in 1927 armed only with talent and charm and brass to match and obtained an interview with Showman S. Z. (Roxy) Rothafel by singing outside Roxy's office door until he admitted him. Roxy put him under contract as one of "Roxy's Gang at the Roxy Theater," and soon thereafter he began radio appearances in which he was an immediate success with his repertoire ranging from black spirituals and folk songs to show tunes and operatic arias.

He began nationwide concert tours in 1930, made his Town Hall debut in 1932 and did 28 concerts with the great George Gershwin in 1934 in which he specialized in songs from "Porgy and Bess," which he later always included as highlights of his concert programs.

Standing six-foot-two with blue eyes, black, wavy hair and a baby face, Melton was a natural for the movies and starred in a number of musicals for Warner Brothers beginning in 1935. But because his all-consuming ambition was to sing in grand opera, he left Hollywood to join the Cincinnati Summer Opera in 1938 and became a member of the Chicago City Opera later that same year; he remained with that organization until he obtained an audition with the Metropolitan in 1942. The Met's Bruno Walter was impressed and asked him to study the piquant role of Tamino, which Melton committed to memory in five days and in which he made his debut to critical acclaim three weeks later.

He performed 15 times a year for the Metropolitan for the next 10 years, and his success was credited with ending the prejudice of that company against the admission of singers from the popular field.

Throughout his ten seasons with the Met he also gave up to fifty concerts yearly throughout the nation and starred in such popular radio shows as the Texaco Star Theater, the Telephone Hour and the Harvest of Stars. After he left the Metropolitan he established a touring nightclub act which enjoyed great success in major cities, and he made an easy transition to television to star on the Ford Festival on the NBC network in 1951 and 1952.

He devoted his spare time to the collection of antique automobiles, fire engines and stagecoaches, and when that collection of more than a hundred vehicles outgrew the confines of his home in Norwich, Connecticut, he established the Melton Museum at Hypoluxo near Palm Beach in 1953. The Museum became one of Florida's major tourist attractions.

Whenever Melton traveled, he extolled the virtues of southern cooking and had a standing order with the Biltmore Hotel for a meal of country ham, blackeyed peas, turnip greens and pot-likker, cornbread and sorghum syrup whenever he visited Atlanta, and he always delighted in hosting his high-toned New York musical colleagues to such gustatory experiences. His pet peeves were improperly cooked collards and cornbread prepared with sugar.

Melton delighted in being compared with both Caruso and Barnum at the same time, and he never hesitated to tell reporters how much he enjoyed singing and the life which went with it.

"Singing is the first thing and the most important thing," he told Atlanta Journal Magazine book editor Frank Daniel in 1948. "I like to please the people who listen to me sing. I'm having a good time and I don't know why I shouldn't admit it."

He died in New York City of lobar pneumonia and was buried in Ocala, Florida.

James Melton

JOHNNY MERCER

Any list of America's ten greatest songwriters would include the name of Johnny Mercer of Savannah, Georgia. Most authorities rank him as the greatest lyricist the nation has produced. A recitation of the titles of his hits beginning with "Lazybones" with Hoagy Carmichael in 1933 and running through "Good Companions" with Andre Previn in 1974 constitutes by itself a graphic history spanning the four momentous decades from the Great Depression to the Space Age.

With 701 published songs, 90 film credits, 6 Broadway musicals, four Academy Awards from 15 nominations and 37 hit Parade songs of which 13 were No. 1, he is Georgia's undisputed premier musician of all times. His life appropriately has been honored by his posthumous induction into the Georgia Music Hall of Fame and the enshrining of his works and memorabilia in the Johnny Mercer Room established in the Georgia State University Library in Atlanta.

Mercer won his first Oscar in 1946 for "On the Atchison, Topeka, and the Sante Fe," written with Harry Warren for MGM's "The Harvey Girls," and repeated in 1951 for "In the Cool, Cool, Cool of the Evening," done with Carmichael for Paramount's "Here Comes the Groom." Then he received two in a row with Henry Mancini for "Moon River," from Paramount's "Breakfast at Tiffany's," in 1961 and "Days of Wine and Roses," from the Warner Brothers film of the same title, in 1962.

Others of his Academy Award nominations include "Jeepers Creepers" in 1939, "Love of My Life" in 1941, "Blues in the Night" in 1942, "That Old Black Magic" in 1943, "My Shining Hour" in 1944, "Ac-Cent-Tchu—Ate the Positive" in 1945, "Somethings's Gotta Give" in 1956, "The Facts of Life" in 1960, "Charade" in 1964, "The Sweetheart Tree" in 1966 and "Life Is What You Make It" in 1971.

He had six straight nominations from 1941 to 1946, four of them consecutive hits written with Harold Arlen who, with

Mancini, was one of his two most successful collaborators. Critics noted that Mercer's Southern background was the perfect complement for Arlen's cantorial one. These two produced some of the enduring classics of American music, particularly "Blues in the Night," for which Arlen persuaded Mercer to move the line "My Momma done told me" up to the opening.

It is impossible to single out any one Mercer song as most popular, but two of his most memorable ones for which he did both the words and music were "I'm an Old Cowhand," from the 1935 movie "Old Man Rhythm," one of the two films in which Johnny appeared, and "G. I. Jive" from World War II.

A reading of the list of his Hit Parade songs between the years of 1935 and 1955 is a nostalgia trip for anyone over 40; in addition to the above-named and the Oscar-winning tunes, the list includes "Eeny Meenie Miney Mo" in 1935; "I'm Building Up to an Awful Letdown," "Goody Goody," "Lost" and "Dream Awhile" in 1936; "Too Marvelous for Words" and "Have You Got Any Castles, Baby?" in 1937; "Bob White, Whatcha Gonna Swing Tonight," "Daydreaming" and "You Must Have Been a Beautiful Baby" in 1938; "Could Be," "Gotta Get Some Shuteye," "And the Angels Sing" (Bing Crosby's favorite) and "Day In — Day Out" in 1939; "Fools Rush In Where Angels Fear to Tread" in 1940; "Tangerine," "I Remember You," "Skylark" and "Dearly Beloved" in 1942; "Laura," "Dream" and "Out of This World" in 1945; "Wait and See" and "Come Rain or Come Shine" in 1946; "Glow Worm" in 1952; "P. S. I Love You" in 1953; and "Autumn Leaves" in 1955.

Among others of his works which have become standards are "Hooray for Hollywood," "Mister Meadowlark," "You Were Never Lovelier," "I'm Old Fashioned," "Hit the Road to Dreamland," "One for My Baby and One More for the Road," "How Little We Know," "I Wonder What Became of Me," "Any Place I Hang My Hat Is Home," "Early Autumn," "When the World Was Young," "Song of India," "Spring, Spring, Spring," "Midnight Sun," "Love in the Afternoon," "If I Had My Druthers," "Satin Doll," "The Bilboa Song," "Emily," "Summer Wind" and "Happy Ever After."

Born to wealth on November 18, 1909, John Herndon Mercer attended a fashionable Virginia prep school and was forced to drop out of college by the bankruptcy of his father's real estate business precipitated by the economic crash of the late 20's. He

149

vowed to himself at the time that he one day would pay off his father's debts, a promise on which he was able to make good in the early 1950's when he sold his interest in Capitol Records, which he founded in the early 40's, and sent a Savannah bank his personal check for $300,000 to reimburse all the creditors or their heirs with interest.

His action was a headline story of its day and further reinforced the reputation Johnny had made for himself as an honorable and affable man liked by everyone, a man who could work successfully with the most temperamental composers and artists and whose trademarks were his cherubic face, broad, gap-toothed grin and the Greek fisherman's cap he loved to wear.

A devotee of jazz and blues from the days when he, his cousin Walter Rivers and their boyhood black friends would sneak into the Negro neighborhood of Savannah to listen to "race" recordings on an old Victrola at Mamie's Record Store, Johnny was cited for his "love of music" in the yearbook of Woodbury Forest Preparatory School, and at the time he left to seek his fortune in New York City at the age of 19, he was an admirer of the music of Louis Armstrong and Paul Whiteman and the plays of Noel Coward; he listed as his heroes Victor Herbert, Irving Berlin, George Gershwin, Walter Donaldson, Gus Kahn, Isham Jones and W. S. Gilbert, whom he called his "idol."

His outgoing personality got him a job as a runner delivering papers and securities on Wall Street, but he hung out on Broadway and around Tin Pan Alley and showed up at every audition of which he learned, including one for "The Garrick Gaieties," where they tried to discourage him by saying they needed songs instead of singers and where he met Songwriter Everett Miller with whom he teamed up to write "Out of Breath and Scared to Death of You," which was incorporated into the show. It became his first published song and led to his first professional job as a contract writer with Miller Music.

He also met and fell in love with one of the dancers in that show, Elizabeth "Ginger" Meehan, whom he married in 1931 in a lifelong union which produced two children, Jeff and Mandy. Ginger and Bob Bach joined in doing his biography entitled "Our Huckleberry Friend" after his death on June 25, 1976.

The biggest disappointment of his career was his failure to do a smash stage musical or to scale the heights of Broadway in the six attempts he made between 1946 and 1963. In 1932 he worked

150

with E. Y. "Yip" Harburg, to whom he later would refer as "my guru," in collaboration with Arlen on the revue "Americana," and Jerome Robbins sent him to London to do one of Lew Leslie's "Blackbirds." He and Arlen wrote "St. Louis Woman" in 1946, but it failed when Lena Horne dropped out after NAACP objections, although it did make a star of Pearl Bailey. He and Robert Emmet Dolan had a flop "Texas, Li'l Darlin'" in 1949, and in 1951 he did both words and music for "Top Banana," an Uncle Miltie takeoff which ran for 350 performances and was released as a film, but which did not achieve major hit status.

His biggest stage success was with "Li'l Abner" in 1956, which he did with Gene de Paul following their triumph with the classic screen musical "Seven Brides for Seven Brothers"; it lasted for 693 performances and was made into a movie. He and Arlen tried again in 1959 with "Saratoga," based on the Edna Ferber book, but it sank under the weight of bad reviews; and a second attempt with Dolan in 1963 with "Foxy," written for Bert Lahr, closed shortly after it moved to New York's Ziegfeld Theater from Alaska. His last effort was his collaboration in England with London Symphony Orchestra Conductor Andre Previn on "The Good Companions" in 1973; it produced some memorable music but was lambasted by London critics for lyrics that were "not British enough."

Mercer's major triumphs were scored in the fields of movies, radio and recording. He got his first big break in 1932 when he won the Pontiac Youth of America Contest to appear on Paul Whiteman's Kraft radio program. Whiteman liked him so much that he kept him on for a year to write, emcee and sing with his orchestra. His success in jointly writing both words and music to "Lazybones" with Carmichael in 1933 and single-handedly producing the hit "I'm an Old Cowhand" for the movie in which he starred with Buddy Rogers in 1935 led to a contract with Warner Brothers and a stint in Hollywood with such greats as Richard Whiting, Harry Warren, Ziggy Elman, Jerome Kern and Gordon Jenkins. With Arlen and Carmichael he produced an unequalled succession of Oscar-winning songs and other hits.

He also was in great demand on radio and, in addition to Whiteman's show, worked on the Benny Goodman Camel Caravan, Bob Crosby's Show, Your Hit Parade, the Pepsodent Show as Bob Hope's replacement (on which he enhanced his identity singing the commercial, "Poor Miriam . . . forgot to use her irium"), his own Johnny Mercer's Music Shop and numerous morale-building broadcasts to the armed forces during World War II.

He joined with songwriter-producer Buddy DeSylva and Hollywood record store owner Glen Wallichs in founding Capitol Records in 1942; he became its first President and built it into the nation's largest recording company by the time he sold out his interest in the early 50's. He not only was one of the most important stars using his own label but also helped make recording greats of such artists as Peggy Lee, Nat "King" Cole, Paul Weston, Paul Whiteman, Stan Kenton, Margaret Whiting, Les Paul and Mary Ford, Ella Mae Morse, Freddy Slack, Bobby Sherwood and the Woody Herman Band. His wife wrote in her book that he quit the business because "the receptionist wouldn't know who he was" when he walked into the office, but his profits made him independent for the remainder of his life and allowed him to pay off his late father's debts.

After musical trends passed him by, he devoted his last years to founding and being first president of the Songwriters' Hall of Fame in New York. He also served as president of the National Academy of Television Arts and Sciences and was a Director of ASCAP. He received the Ed Wynn Humanitarian Award, was commissioned an Admiral in the Georgia Navy, served on the White House Record Library Commission and was proudest of the honor bestowed upon him by the Board of Commissioners of Chatham County in changing the name of the Back River in his home county to that of Moon River. His hobby was riding trains, which he did as frequently as possible, both coast-to-coast and to and from his beloved Savannah, to which he went often to refresh himself.

There have been many attempts to analyze the secret of his success in writing memorable and enduring lyrics. Fred Astaire attributed it to the fact that Mercer had "the common touch expressed in uncommon lyrics." Mel Torme said it was that he wrote in "the idiom of his decades." President Gerald Ford said it was that "his phrases were full of affection for people everywhere." Irving Berlin, who would have to be his closest rival for the title of "Greatest American Songwriter," attributed it to his high literacy in knowing when and when not to use "all those six and seven-syllable words" and the fact that "he's very sentimental and knows how to use tender corn." Or, as was stated at the

ASCAP Mercer Tribute in 1978: "Song was his life, and his life was a song — 'free and easy' was his style, but hard-working professionalism was his excellence. He approached romance and farce with a wry, fresh viewpoint. He always held something back, too. His lyrics will never dull from outmoded mawkishness. He was the greatest of American lyricists."

Whatever the reason, he managed to capture the soul of America with words and music and, had none of his illustrious predecessors and successors ever existed, he single-handedly would have put the State of Georgia into the pages of the musical history of the world.

Johnny Mercer
Courtesy of Frederick C. Baldwin

Ronnie Milsap

RONNIE MILSAP

The talents of blind troubadour Ronnie Milsap fortunately are sufficiently colossal to be spread over the three states of North Carolina, Georgia and Tennessee, which all claim him, with enough left over for the remaining 47 to join them in applauding this most admired and respected entertainer of the second half of the Twentieth Century.

Born blind by congenital glaucoma in Robbinsville, North Carolina, on January 10, 1944, and abandoned by his mother as an infant, Ronnie was reared by his grandfather, Homer Frisby, in Hayesville, North Carolina, just across the state line from Young Harris, Georgia, where he later graduated from Young Harris College.

His musical genius was discovered and developed with classical training at the Morehead School for the Blind in Raleigh, North Carolina, where he was a violin virtuoso at the age of seven, a master of the piano at eight, an accomplished guitarist at 12 and a performer on all instruments except brass which he found "boring" by the time of his graduation.

But it was in Georgia where he decided to pursue his personal choice of a musical career rather than the legal one picked for him by North Carolina authorities who awarded him a full scholarship to attend law school at Emory University. It was in Georgia where he met and married Joyce Reeves, who has been his adoring wife for 20 years and who became his "eyes." Ronnie and Joyce, the daughter of a Douglas, Georgia, chicken farmer, lived on the edge of poverty out of a motel in Gainesville, and he "paid his dues" by playing whatever kind of music was needed in whatever kind of club or dive in the Atlanta area that would hire him. It was in Georgia, too, where he developed into the anomaly of a white man who could sing rhythm and blues songs like a black man and who played with such great black artists as Jerry Butler, Jackie Wilson, Ben E. King and B. B. King at the Royal Peacock on Atlanta's Auburn Avenue. His talent won him a contract with Scepter Records for which he recorded the Ashford and Simpson single "Never Had It So Good," which reached No. 5 on the R&B Charts in 1966 and brought him engagements on the black circuit, including playing at the Old Howard Theater in Washington, D. C., with stars like Smokey Robinson and The Miracles and Little Anthony and the Imperials.

It was fellow Georgian Chips Moman, composer of "Luckenbach, Texas," which later was to become the anthem of Willie, Waylon and the other outlaws, who lured Ronnie to Memphis, Tennessee, in 1969, to work as a recording session keyboardist by day for big names like Elvis Presley, Petula Clark, B. J. Thomas and Dionne Warwick and to perform by night at T. J.'s, the famous Memphis hang-out. It was Ronnie who did the background piano work for Elvis' recordings of "In the Ghetto," "Suspicious Minds" and "Kentucky Rain," and he so impressed Presley that he soon became "The King's" favorite pianist for his private parties at Graceland.

However, he was dissatisfied with his inability not only to get anyone to record his music but also to establish his own identity, and he was seeking ways to get back into his first love of country music when he came to the attention of Jack Johnson, Charley Pride's manager, who told Pride about him. Charley caught his act when Ronnie was playing in Los Angeles in 1970 and called him to tell him, "Come to Nashville. I'll help you if I can." Thus came about the supreme irony in Ronnie's odyssey to super-stardom — he, a white man whose major credential was being able to sing like a black man, was being given his big boost up the ladder to success by a black man who already had achieved his stardom by singing like a white man.

It was not a pleasant or easy transition, however, because Milsap had signed a long-term contract with T. J.'s and was unable to obtain his release from it. When he decided to leave anyway, he was sued and he and Joyce lost everything, including the home they had bought in Memphis, and they arrived in Nashville in 1972 as broke as the day they first hit the road in Georgia.

Fortunately, Roger Miller signed him as resident singer for the rooftop lounge of his King of the Road Motor Inn; the compensation included a room for them and their infant son, Todd, and Pride and Jackson made good on their promise to arrange a contract with RCA, the company for which Pride recorded.

His first single, "I Hate You," made the charts in 1973, and the same year his second, "The Girl That Waits on Tables," rose to the Top 10. In 1974 he scored the first of the twenty No. 1 hits he was to do over the next eight years with "Pure Love," the composition of a struggling young songwriter named Eddie Rabbit. He had two other No. 1's that year, "I'd Be a Legend in My Time" and "Please Don't Tell Me How the Story Ends." The latter won for him the first of his three Grammys for Best Male Country Vocal Performance, the Country Music Association's Male Vocalist of the Year Award and Billboard Magazine's Best New Male Artist Award. Coming within two years of his entry into the country and western music field, the awards brought comments of "overnight success" and criticism of "failure to pay his dues" from the unknowing, prompting Joyce to observe: "If he's an overnight success, it was a long night."

He went on the road with Pride and remained with him for more than a year before striking out on the concert circuit on his own. He was invited to join the Grand Ole Opry in 1976 and proceeded to turn out an unending string of Top 10 hits including "Too Late to Worry, Too Blue to Cry," "Daydreams About Night Things" and "She Even Woke Me Up to Say Goodbye"; "What Goes On When the Sun Goes Down" and "Stand by My Woman Man" in 1976; "It Was Almost Like a Song" and "What a Difference You've Made in My Life" in 1977; "Let's Take the Long Way Around the World" and "Back on My Mind Again" in 1978; "Nobody Likes Sad Songs" and "In No Time at All" in 1979; "Why Don't You Spend the Night," "My Heart" and "Smokey Mountain Rain" in 1980; "Am I Losing You," "There's No Gettin' Over Me" and "I Wouldn't Have Missed It for the World" in 1981; and "Any Day Now," "I Love New Orleans Music" and "Inside" in 1982. He also did the movie soundtrack for "Bronco Billy," which included the hit "Cowboys and Clowns," and has been in great demand as a guest on all major television shows.

His second and third Grammys (out of five nominations) came in 1976 for "I'm a Stand By My Woman Man" and in 1981 for "There's No Gettin' Over Me." He holds more awards from the Country Music Association than any other single male artist and is the only three-time winner of both the CMA Vocalist and Album of the Year Awards, having received the former in 1974,

1976 and 1977 and the latter in 1975, 1977 and 1978. In 1977 he swept the Country Music Association Awards when he received the Awards for Entertainer, Male Vocalist and Album of the Year, and he holds virtually every other country music award for which he is eligible, including Billboard Magazine's Bill Williams Memorial Award as Artist of the Year in 1976, Special "Breakthrough" Award for Outstanding Artist Achievement in 1981, Male Singles Artist Awards for 1976 and 1980 and Overall Singles Artist Award for 1976.

He received the Record World Top Male Vocalist Award in 1976 and Male Country Single Artist Award in 1980 and the Cashbox Magazine Most Artistic Achievement and Male Country Singles Artists Awards in 1979, Male Singles Artist Award in 1980 and Male Vocalist of the Year for Country Single Award in 1981 and Top Male Vocalist in 1982. He has been accredited on RCA with six Gold and one Platinum Albums and the only Gold Braille Album ever to be awarded to any artist.

Although he is sightless and has known poverty both as a child and adult, Milsap refuses to write or sing sad songs. His outlook is positive; his personality, outgoing; and his only peeves are those with journalists and talk show hosts who want to discuss his feelings about his blindness and fans who invade the privacy of his home in the fashionable Nashville suburb near the Governor's Mansion and the homes of Minnie Pearl and Tammy Wynette. Having never been sighted, he does not miss what he cannot comprehend and has trained himself to be so self-sufficient that, having paced it off in advance, he can work at ease all over a stage without stumbling or faltering, and one of his favorite "stunts" is to astound his audiences by walking to the edge of the stage and teetering on the brink while cracking jokes about the time he fell into the orchestra pit and "saw stars."

At the beginning of his career he was addicted to rhinestone studded costumes in flashy colors, but in recent years has replaced the glitz with open-necked shirts, embroidered jeans and monogrammed glasses. His musical styles have become softer and more subdued also; and, while his albums and programs still have a mix of country, rock, gospel and rhythm and blues, he is tending more and more to do mainstream pop songs with broad appeal and is considering assembling a large orchestra to back his Las Vegas style reviews. Versatile is the word most often used to describe his music, and he says his one criterion for selecting any song he performs is "Is it people music?"

Critics generally concede that had he stayed with the Mozart and Bach on which he was trained he could have been another Van Cliburn. However, he doubts such ever would have happened, noting that he was suspended several times at blind school for playing Jerry Lee Lewis' "Whole Lot of Shakin' " instead of the "Minuet in G" and that his teachers finally relented and let him and three other blind students form a rock group known as "The Apparitions." He says he regards music "as my identity in this world"; he calls himself a "modern day Huck Finn" and explains, "He envisioned everything in his head. So do I." Most who know of him and his fabulous talent and success over great odds would say the best description of him is the title of his smash hit — A Legend in His Own Time.

JESSYE NORMAN

With a silvery voice covering a fantastic three-octave range from E-flat below Middle C to E-flat above High C, Jessye Norman of Augusta, Georgia, was acclaimed throughout Europe as the greatest operatic soprano since Kirsten Flagstad and Birgit Nilsson for 13 years before her American debut, but in 1983 she made up for lost time at home by receiving two nominations for Grammy Awards and joining the New York Metropolitan Opera for its centenary season.

The daughter of the late Silas Norman, an Augusta insurance executive and one of the early black candidates for public office in that city, Jessye began singing in the Mt. Calvary Baptist Church at the age of seven. Her father was Sunday School Superintendent there for 28 years. She won a number of talent contests and participated in sit-ins in Augusta while attending Lucy Laney High School and pursued her college studies in music first at Howard University and then at the University of Michigan under the tutelage of French baritone Pierre Bernac. In 1968 she won a singing competition in Munich, Germany, and received a three-year contract with the Deutsche Oper in Berlin, where she made her operatic debut in the role of Elisabeth in "Tannhauser." However, after a recital in London, she decided her voice was not suited for Wagner and asked for her release. She settled in England, where she wrote for The London Times and developed a performing and recording repertoire of parts ranging from contralto and mezzo to lyric or dramatic soprano. Her death scene as Dido in the BBC Promenade Festival performance of "The Trojans" by Berlioz, which packed Royal Albert Hall, was acclaimed by British critics as "ravishing, grandiose, luminous and voluptuous." She also won highest praise for her lieder recitals at the Edinburgh Festival and her Haydn and early Verdi.

In 1982 she was named Musical America's "Musician of the Year" and appeared on the cover of International Directory of the Performing Arts. She was also nominated for Grammy Awards in two categories.

REX NELON

For 20 years Rex Nelon's was the booming bass that stirred audiences for the LeFevres and, since forming his own Rex Nelon Singers eight years ago, he and his group based in Smyrna, Georgia, have been winning awards right and left, including a Dove Award, Gospel Music's equivalent of the Grammy, for "One Step Closer," the Best Traditional Gospel Album of the Year in 1981. They have had a total of 10 Dove Nominations since 1977 as well as being the Grammy Nominee for Gospel Album and Best Gospel Performance Traditional for their "Feelings" in 1980.

The Southern Gospel Music Association voted the Nelon Singers the Best Mixed Gospel Group of the Year in 1982 and its members hold the following Singing News Fan Awards: Rex, Favorite Gospel Bass Singer, 1980; Kelly Nelon-Thompson, Queen of Gospel Music, 1980 and 1981; and Tenor Jerry Thompson, featured on Song of the Year, 1981. The group holds Fan Awards for Song of the Year, "Come Morning," for 1980 and Favorite Group of the Year, Number One Vote Getter and Favorite Song of the Year, "Sweet Beulah Land," for 1981. All individual singers as well as the band were nominees for best in their categories in 1982.

The Rex Nelon Singers record for Canaan Records, a division of Word, Inc., the largest Christian Music Record Company in the world.

GRAM PARSONS

Gram Parsons did not live to see fruition of the objective which was the obsession of his short, tragic life — the unification of all segments of the pop music audience into the country rock movement of which he is regarded as a principal pioneer. But the memory of this haunted young musical genius who grew up in Waycross, Georgia, and whose body was stolen and cremated by friends after his untimely death in California at the age of twenty-six is being perpetuated by his protege Emmylou Harris who has championed his cause, popularized his music and achieved in her career the fame which was denied him in his.

He was born Cecil Conner on November 5, 1946 in Winter-haven, Florida, the son of country singer and songwriter "Coon Dog" Conner who committed suicide after moving his family to Waycross where he operated a packing plant. His mother married wealthy New Orleans businessman Robert Parsons who changed his name to Gram Parsons and lavished on him the trust fund which financed the dissolute life-style which killed him.

After mastering the piano and guitar at early ages, he ran away from home at fourteen, was playing in a folk band with Jim Stafford in Greenwich Village at sixteen, passed the entrance examination to Harvard at seventeen only to drop out after five months because of his preoccupation with LSD trips, and formed his own band, the International Submarine Band, which distinguished itself with one purist country album in Lee Hazlewood's label which flopped and now is a rare collector's item.

Gram migrated to California where he joined the acclaimed rock group, the Byrds, and with Chris Hillman convinced the band to experiment with country music and to record "Sweetheart of the Rodeo," the first real country rock album which brought the Byrds an invitation to appear on the Grand Ole Opry where they sang Gram's own composition "Hickory Wind," which later was to be featured with great impact by Emmylou in her 1979 album, "Blue Kentucky Girl."

The Byrds left him stranded in England after he objected to accepting an invitation to tour South Africa and he formed friendships with Keith Richards and Mick Jagger of The Rolling Stones which continued until his death. Jagger wrote the song "Wild Horses" about and for him, as later did Emmylou with her composition "Boulder to Birmingham."

In 1969 he and Hillman formed the landmark country-rock group, "The Flying Burrito Brothers," whose first LP, "The Guilded Palace of Sin," which featured their joint composition, "Sin City" won critical acclaim, including the praise of Bob Dylan, but was too far ahead of its time for acceptance by the majority of either country or rock fans. Gram did three albums including some of his best songs on the one entitled "Guilded Palace" before leaving the Burritos to concentrate on solo work after being severely injured in a motorcycle accident in 1970.

Although getting more into drugs and drink, he was given a contract by Warner Reprise on the strength of a possible album with Merle Haggard, but Haggard backed out. Gram assembled a new band featuring Harris, the Alabama girl he had met while she was singing folk songs in and around Baltimore and Washington, D. C. and whose high soaring voice was just what Parsons needed for perfect harmony for his country singing. They did two albums of mostly Gram songs, "GP" and "Grievous Angel," neither of which were successful, but which gave Emmylou a treasure of future songs for her own career.

After his wife left him, he died presumably of a heart attack at Joshua Tree Inn in California's Yucca Valley while on a weekend of drinking and drugs with a group of friends. Before an autopsy could be held his body was stolen from the Los Angeles International Airport by his manager and friends and, in accordance with a previous understanding was cremated at the base of Cap Rock in Joshua Tree National Park before it could be sent home.

Parsons in death has become a cult figure and Emmylou has included at least one of his songs in each of her albums and never fails to tell her audiences that they should "look behind me to all that was going on with Gram and the Burritos." As for Gram, he said while working with the Burritos that all he wanted to do was "take the sweetness and down-home feeling of country music and create goose bumps."

OJEDA PENN

A principal innovator with outstanding talent in the development of the growing jazz recording industry in Atlanta is pianist Ojeda Penn, who moved to the city in 1967 and released his first highly acclaimed album, "Happiness," through Aapogee Studio in 1980.

A virtuoso on both acoustic and electric pianos as well as the synthesizer, Ojeda combines the three in easy transitions to produce melodic styles and modern instrumentation ranked among the best of contemporary jazz. He is popular on the Atlanta club circuit, and his keyboard techniques have been compared to those of jazz artists Duke and McCoy Tyner.

Former Atlanta Mayor Maynard Jackson called his recordings "joyous and sensitive," and his arranging, composing and orchestrating abilities have prompted critics to label him "one of Atlanta's leading jazz artists."

165

HANK PENNY

Although he objects to the term and is critical of those to whom it currently applies, Herbert Clayton "Hank" Penny was a musical outlaw before being an outlaw was cool. And because he was a rebel with a streak of puritanism, his musical ideas were before their time early in his career and out of date later in his career.

Consequently, all but the most avid country music buffs revere Bob Wills and love Roy Clark but are unaware that it was Penny who perfected the western swing techniques of Wills and taught Clark much of what he knows about guitar picking and country comedy.

But one place where he still is remembered and beloved is in Atlanta and the area covered by the Voice of the South, radio station WSB, over which Penny and his Radio Cowboys were stars of the daily noontime Crossroads Follies from 1938 to 1943.

A young, mostly self-taught, ambitious Birmingham miner's son fresh from a stint with Lew Childre of station WWL in New Orleans where he became an ardent fan of Wills' music, Hank put together a new sound in Atlanta, Georgia. It was built around Noel Boggs, a jazz-minded steel guitarist whom he lured away from New Orleans, and Georgian Boudleaux Bryant, a classical violinist with the Atlanta Civic Symphony whom he converted to a lover of country music. And it was punctuated by the percussion of his own distinctive rhythm guitar tuned an octave higher than the normal G-string instrument.

It was also at this time that Penny began alternating his new swing-style music with his own brand of country comedy for which he would later bill himself as "That Plain Ol' Country Boy from Rimlap, Alabama."

Penny's dream of going to the Grand Ole Opry was shattered by the Opry's refusal to accept Boggs' electric steel guitar because it was not in keeping with traditional country music, an irony underscored by the fact that Penny today criticizes the Opry for being "too hokey" and endangering the more traditional forms through the "overproduction" of the Nashville Sound.

He and his band did record a number of the songs they made popular at WSB for ARC, Okeh and Columbia Records, including "Won't You Ride in My Little Red Wagon," "Hawaiian Honeymoon" and "Lonesome Trail Blues" before disbanding because of the draft.

Declared 4-F, Hank left Atlanta and went to Cincinnati in 1943 and became the top performer on the WLW Boone Country Jamboree and Midwestern Hayride. There he formed a close friendship with the great Merle Travis, who later persuaded him to move to the west coast. He also began a stormy relationship with Syd Nathan, who signed him as a charter artist for his King Records where he cut his greatest hits and with whom Hank broke in 1947 because of a demand that Hank record songs which he felt were "too risque."

While on the west coast, he made four musical western movies with Charles Starrett and returned to radio with his Penny Serenade Show and as a comedian on ABC Radio's weekly Roundup Time. He got into television as a stand-up western comic first with Spade Cooley, whose music he also admired and emulated, and then with Dude Martin as well as with his own Hank Penny Show in Culver City. His new band, the Penny Serenaders and then the California Cowhands, gained a reputation as one of the finest western swing bands in America. It featured a female singer, Jaye P. Morgan, who later became famous as a pop singer.

He recorded the classic "Steel Guitar Stomp" and "Remington Ride" and had his biggest hits with "Get Yourself a Redhead" in 1946 and "Bloodshot Eyes" in 1949. He also was a partner in "The Palomino" nightclub in North Hollywood which he gave away before it became the foremost country music club it is today.

He moved to Las Vegas in 1954 where he played both jazz and country music at the Golden Nugget for seven years. It was a magnet for young country talent, the most famous of whom was Roy Clark.

In 1961 Hank Penny came back to Atlanta, where he had first become so popular, to record an instrumental jazz LP for NRC.

From 1963 to 1970 he lived in Carson City and worked mostly at Harrah's. Then he tried to crash Nashville for the second time,

167

and the producers of "Hee Haw" turned him down because they said they already had a guitar-playing comedian in Hank's protege, Roy Clark.

A broken man, he spent the next three years in Wichita, Kansas, as a disc jockey at station WFRM owned by a former western band leader who was an old friend.

In 1975 he and his fifth wife, Shari, returned to the San Fernando Valley where he now lives in semi-retirement, working in an occasional movie and dreaming of forming another band to resurrect the greatness which would have been his but for the fate of timing and his uncompromising stubbornness.

Hank Penny
Courtesy of the Country Music Foundation Library and Media Center

PIANO RED
William (Willie Lee) Perryman

Ask any person on the street who recorded the first rock 'n' roll record and odds are you will get one of three responses — Bill Haley and the Comets, Elvis or the Beatles — all wrong. The correct answer is William (Willie Lee) Perryman of Hampton, Georgia, a black rhythm and blues and barrelhouse pianist who, as Piano Red, helped make old Underground Atlanta famous with his performaces at Mulenbrink's Saloon and, as Dr. Feelgood, is one of the best-known and most-sought-after acts on the college fraternity circuit.

Red, as he prefers to be called, cut that pioneer disc for RCA Victor and Producer Steve Sholes (who later made a rock recording star of Elvis) in 1950. It was a 78 rpm titled "Rockin' With Red (Rock, Rock, Rock)" which earned Red a gold record in 1951 but, because it was regarded as a "race" record which was not played on white radio stations of the period, it was listed on the rhythm and blues charts and overlooked by rock historians. In fact, it was so much a progenitor of rock that it was a hit before Disc Jockey Allen Freed took the term "rock 'n' roll" from the idiom of the black streets and introduced it into the national vocabulary on a white-oriented station.

But history is being corrected thanks to the efforts of The Lowery Group and Producer Sonny Limbo who issued an album of Red's best-known songs in 1978 titled "First Piece of The Rock" and including a new performance of the 1950 original and the Georgia Music Hall of Fame which inducted him into membership in 1983, thus immortalizing him in the company of such other black Georgia musical greats as Ray Charles and Dr. Thomas A. Dorsey. His work and style also has attracted the attention and admiration of Mick Jagger and the Rolling Stones who often visit and consult with him and one of his minor hits of the early 60's, "Mr. Moonlight," was covered and made even more popular by the Beatles.

William (Willie Lee) Perryman

Following up on the success of his original rock disc, Red had a string of R & B hits which included "Right String Baby But the Wrong Yo-Yo," "Red's Boogie" and "Laying The Boogie." His recording successes led to his popular live radio shows on Station WAOK in Atlanta and his album, "Dr. Feelgood," and subsequent nightclub act, "Dr. Feelgood and the Interns," made him and his band in great demand on college campuses, a popularity which continues to the present. All of his recordings were even more successful in Europe than the United States and he is a popular concert performer in England, France, Germany, Holland and Switzerland. His crossover popularity soared as his Underground Atlanta performances won him widespread acclaim and following among white adult audiences in Georgia's Capital City.

Red was born the son of a sharecropper on a farm near Hampton in Henry County and developed his innovative style of blues and rock piano playing and song writing and singing in the honky tonks of Decatur Street in segregated Atlanta. Although he is now approaching the age of 75, he remains a vigorous and active performer who is offered more bookings than he can accept.

"Time has not diminished his technical skills, willingness to perform as often as need be, and more importantly, his joie de vivre," said Limbo who feels that history's temporary oversight of Red's pioneering has been rectified and his place in history has been assured as "the grandfather of rock 'n' roll."

DIANE PFEIFFER

Blonde Diane Pfeiffer studied to be a chemist at Merrimee College in her hometown of Saint Louis, Missouri, but the only formula she discovered was how to write and sing country songs which she used when she moved to Marietta, Georgia.

She won an invitation to perform at Opryland in a contest sponsored by Atlanta country music station WPLO which led to a job singing back-up for Tammy Wynette, a songwriting and recording contract with Capitol Records and an award as Georgia Songwriter of the Year in 1982.

The 32-year-old Pfeiffer put her single "Free to Be Lonely Again" on the national country charts in 1980, had an album produced by Larry Butler, and had her songs recorded by Roy Clark, Dottie West, Billy Jo Spears, Debby Boone and Johnny Mathis. The latter two placed high in the charts with Debby's cover of Diane's single and Johnny with her "Perfect Fool."

In 1981 her "Play Something We Could Love To" made the Top 40 in country music, and she won the second of her two regional Emmys for songs she has written for commercial television. The Georgia Songwriters Association gave her its top award in 1982.

RILEY PUCKETT

Though they may not remember his name, there are few Americans over the age of fifty who cannot recall being enthralled at one time or another in their youth by the lyric tenor recordings of Georgia's Riley Puckett or being hummed to sleep to the tune of his "Rock-a-Bye-Baby."

The "granddaddy" of the crooners, the first of the recorded yodelers and the originator of the wild bass run guitar style which was the forerunner of bluegrass and rock techniques, Puckett was one of the first superstars of the infantile recording industry in the 1920's. Probably the most versatile artist of his time, he established himself as a virtuoso instrumentalist, composer, folk-singer, balladeer and minstrel.

Born May 7, 1894, in Alpharetta, Georgia, and blinded at the age of three months by the wrong medication used for a minor eye ailment, George Riley Puckett graduated from the Georgia Academy for the Blind and learned to play the five-string banjo at the age of twelve and then the guitar in order to have a means of livelihood.

As a performer he attracted a following with contemporaries like Fiddlin' John Carson, Gid Tanner and Clayton McMichen. He appeared on Atlanta's radio station WSB in its infancy in 1922 and played with Carson on "Little Old Log Cabin in the Lane" before any recordings were made. Tanner invited him to go with him to New York to make the first recordings of southern artists for Capitol Records to offset those made a year earlier by Carson by Okeh Records and then to join him as one of The Skillet Lickers, the wild Georgia string band which dominated the recording industry through the 1930's.

Puckett billed himself as "King of the Hill Billies" (two words), toured the United States, performed on the Grand Ole Opry and, in addition to WSB, appeared on such pioneer radio stations as WCKY in Covington, Kentucky, WLS in Chicago, WSM in Nashville and WMAZ in Macon, Georgia. Columbia Records so valued his services that the firm gave him and his wife, Blanche, a honeymoon trip to New York in June 1925 and presented him with a big phonograph and a thousand records as a wedding gift.

All the band members agreed that it was Puckett's singing more than anything else that made the records sell, and it was his incomparable back-up style with the guitar that gave the band its unique sound. He was one of the original five-finger pickers, a style used by the finest guitarists of today, and he set the trend for heavy contrapuntal bass runs which later developed into bluegrass.

He made frequent use of double or quadruple-time runs with the thumb pick held with thumb and forefinger and used the flat pick in the way now emulated by Doc Watson; he shunned chromatic notes in favor of clear, easily heard single-note work. He developed the devices of hesitating so that one of the four basic beats came half a beat late and of strumming the strings upward. His simple solo style is characterized as "pre-Carter Family" to distinguish it from Maybelle Carter's bass melody notes and up-and-down brushing technique.

His singing style was heavily influenced by blues and pop singers and, at times, showed considerable black influence also; and, while he was most noted for his sweet spellbinding tenor, he had a tremendous range and could sing any four parts of a quartet. Like Jimmie Rodgers, whom he predated as a recording yodeler by three years, he could sing a blues or pop song without sounding as out-of-place as did many of his "hillbilly" contemporaries. After the final disbandment of The Skillet Lickers in 1934, he shifted his recording repertoire from essentially traditional to mostly popular hit tunes. He had moved close to the mainstream of northern urban popular music by the time of his untimely death from blood poisoning in East Point, Georgia in 1946.

His classic, "Sleep Baby Sleep," which also is known as "Rock All Our Babies to Sleep" and "Rock-a-Bye-Baby," was recorded September 10, 1924, and featured the first recorded yodeling. He did a bottle-neck style recording of "John Henry" and had an extensive repertoire of familiar lyrical songs and fiddle tunes like "Little Brown Jug," and "Ida Red;" he made ballads out of original folksongs like "Frankie and Johnny," "Bully of the Town," and "Casey Jones."

He recorded new ballads like Bob Miller's "Twenty-One

174

Years" and Carson Robinson's "Altoona Freight Wreck." He did the traditional "Prisoner's Song" as "All Bound Down in Prison" and wrote "Put My Little Shoes Away," "Columbus Stockade Blues," "Ada from Decatur" and many more. He made a whole nation, particularly the women, grow sentimental with such perennial favorites as "Silver Threads Among the Gold," "Down by the Old Mill Stream," "Wait Till the Sun Shines, Nellie," "Old Spinning Wheel in the Parlor" and scores of others which today, trigger nostalgia in the over-fifty age group.

Probably no artist of his era has had as many of his songs played throughout the United States by country musicians nor has had more hits which always will be country and western standards than this blind genius.

Riley Puckett
Courtesy of the Country Music Foundation Library and Media Center

Otis Redding

OTIS REDDING

Otis Redding of Macon, Georgia, who perished at the age of 26 in a tragic airplane crash in 1967, probably did more in his brief but brilliant, career as the writer and singer of sentimental soul ballads to build a bridge between black and white music in America than any other performer. As Jerry Wexler of Atlantic Records put it in 1968: "Otis is tremendously responsible for the fact that . . . the young white audience now digs soul the way the black does."

Redding, who was born in Dawson, Georgia, on September 9, 1941, decided after his family moved to Macon that becoming an entertainer was the one way he could escape the dead-end, lower-class existence into which he had been born and he set out to develop himself along the lines of his idols, Sam Cooke and fellow Maconite Little Richard.

He cut a Little Richard-styled number, "Shout Bamalama," for Bethlehem Records in 1960 which went nowhere, but he began paying his dues as a "gofer" and sometimes-performer for Macon's Johnny Jenkins and the Pinetoppers. He got his big break at a recording session for Stax Records in Memphis, Tennessee, to which he had driven the group in his role as Jenkins' chauffeur/valet in the spring of 1963.

When the Pinetoppers wound up with forty minutes of recording time remaining, someone suggested that Otis sing, and Stax President Jim Stewart agreed. He started out with a Little Richard-type number, but Stewart stopped him and said the last thing the world needed was another Little Richard; and he suggested instead that he sing something slow. Redding responded with a rendition of his own "These Arms of Mine" about which Stewart was mildly enthusiastic and agreed to record and release it. After a slow start, when it eventually rose to No. 20 on the rhythm and blues charts and sold 750,000 copies, it put the shy, but ambitious, 21-year-old Redding on the road to stardom.

Stewart signed Redding to a long-term contract and created a new label, Volt Records, for his release, which found increasing favor with black record buyers and concert goers. When his "Mr. Pitiful" reached No. 10 in 1965, it gave him the name by which he was thereafter known because of the pleading urgency of his soul ballads characterized by sentimental lyrics usually imploring a girlfriend to forgive or come back to him.

Two other singles that year — the slow and aching "I've Been Loving You Too Long" and the classic soul shaker "Respect" —established him as a star. His version of "Respect" went to No. 4 R & B and No. 35 Pop, but the general public really learned who Otis Redding was when Aretha Franklin covered it and carried it to a smash No. 1 two years later.

The advent of the Rolling Stones gave him and modern soul a further boost when that group covered his slow and sad "Pain in My Heart," and he reciprocated by covering their "Satisfaction." That latter experience gave rise to the rumor that Redding was the original author of "Satisfaction" and had sold it to the Stones for $50. The truth of the matter, however, was that neither Redding nor any of the people at Stax/Volt Records could decipher Mick Jagger's lyrics from the 45 RPM recording of it they had bought; so Otis wrote his own different version. Whatever the case, the Redding cut soared to No. 4 and propelled him in another big leap into the white market.

He became in great demand on the black concert circuit and was said to have Harlem and Watts "locked up," but he refused to follow the more commercial style of superstars like James Brown. Redding insisted that the stomp beat and communication had to be the predominant features of modern soul and that his songs were going to be simple, direct, honest and concise. The critics said his style reached "artistic fruition" in late 1966 with his album "The Otis Redding Dictionary of Soul," which was pronounced the "best example of modern soul ever recorded" and proved that assessment by making it with the pop audience.

He stuck with his determination not to change his music and proved the wisdom of his judgment with his success with soul ballads like "Try a Little Tenderness," blues like "Hawg for You" and the revival of the Beatles' "Day Tripper." The only concession he made to the more traditional format was with his No. 16 "Shake" in 1967. That same year he formed his own record company, Jotis, and his own music publishing firm, Redwal, and produced his protege, Arthur Conley, in a Gold Record and No.

2 hit, "Sweet Soul Music," which they co-wrote with Sam Cooke.

His overseas record sales topped even those in the United States, and France rated him one of the world's top singers in its polls for both 1966 and 1967. England's Melody Maker Magazine's naming him Top Male Singer of 1967 in that country dethroned Elvis Presley's eight-year reign with that title. He made several appearances on Dick Clark's "Where the Action Is" and on a number of other major TV shows, went on a month-long R & B tour which grossed more than $250,000 and was the star of the Monterey Pop Festival of 1967. The demands upon his schedule became so great that he purchased a twin-engine Beechcraft to facilitate meeting them, and it was that plane which carried him to his death into the icy waters of Lake Monona while enroute to a concert in Madison, Wisconsin, on December 10, 1967. The crash claimed the lives of all but one member of his musical group, Ben Cauley of Memphis, who heard two cries for help but was unable to save anyone else except himself.

Three days before the tragedy, Otis recorded the song he had written with Steve Crooper, "(Sittin' On) The Dock of the Bay," in Memphis. Released a month after his death, it went to No. 1 on both the R & B and Pop Charts and sold more than four million records; it won Redding two posthumous Grammy Awards in 1968 for Best Male Rhythm and Blues Vocal Performance and Best Rhythm and Blues Song. An album of the same title went to No. 4, and seven other songs issued posthumously all made the charts, including No. 6 "I've Got Dreams to Remember" and No. 10's "The Happy Song" and the cover of James Brown's "Papa's Got a Brand New Bag."

Through the work of Aretha Franklin and contemporaries, the crossover trends started by Redding became the new wave which has erased many of the boundaries separating pop and soul music and accelerated the merger of black and white music into a truly-integrated American art form.

Jerry Reed

JERRY REED

"Hearing Things" would get most people a trip to the funny farm. But when Jerry Reed "kept hearing things in my head," he translated them into the hot licks which earned him a one-way ticket out of the poverty of the Atlanta Exposition Cotton Mill Village to worldwide acclaim as the "Guitar Man" who has written more than 400 songs and to Burt Reynolds' sidekick in the movies.

Born Jerry Reid Hubbard on March 20, 1937, he developed his unique "Finger-picking" style of playing on a beat-up guitar that his mother bought for him for seven dollars when he was five years old. She taught him his first chords while he was sitting on the stovewood box in the family kitchen. He dropped out of school to supplement the family income by tending looms in the cotton mill by day and to perfect his picking technique, usually for free, in the gin mills of the area by night.

He might still be a "lint head" but for a policeman friend who introduced him at the age of sixteen to Bill Lowery. The Atlanta music mogul was impressed by both his enthusiasm and his resemblance to the late James Dean and took him to Hollywood in 1955 where Lowery persuaded Capitol Records Executive Ken Nelson to put him under contract.

In California Jerry cut some "rockabilly" tracks and wrote "Crazy Legs," which Gene Vincent recorded in 1956. But mostly he was frustrated and discouraged until his two-year stint in the service when the Army put him in its Circle A Wranglers, a country group it used for recruiting promotion.

During this time he wrote an instrumental number which was recorded by Chet Atkins, who invited him to come to Nashville to work as a session man after his discharge. When he had trouble limiting himself to the discipline of Army life, Atkins urged him to write the things he heard in his head.

In 1961, he established himself as a coming song writer when another native Georgian, Brenda Lee, chose his "That's All You

181

Gotta Do" to be her hit record of "I'm Sorry." He followed that with the two minor hits of "Goodnight Irene" and "Hully Gully Guitars."

He was signed as a solo act by RCA in 1965 and produced a first album called "The Unbelievable Guitar and Voice of Jerry Reed." Jerry has said that he found the album embarrassing, but it contained the rocking "Guitar Man" which Elvis Presley recorded and made a big hit in 1967 with Reed playing the guitar, an accomplishment which gave him the "Guitar Man" handle by which he continues to be known.

Presley scored another success with Jerry's "U. S. Male," and further Reed hits written for others included "A Thing Called Love" by Johnny Cash, "I Promise" by Tom Jones and "If It Comes To That" by Englebert Humperdinck.

Jerry's own recordings then became hot sellers: "Tupelo Mississippi" in 1967, "Remembering" in 1968, "Are You from Dixie" in 1969, "Talk About the Good Times" and "Georgia Sunshine" in 1970. In the latter part of 1970 he came out with the hit "Amos Moses," which made the Top Ten and brought him a nomination for Instrumentalist of the Year by the Country Music Association. His recording of "When You're Hot You're Hot" was a Number One Country Song in 1971 and won him a Grammy as Top Country Vocalist in 1976, and his "Lord, Mr. Ford" reached the top in 1973.

He had won the first of his two Grammys in 1970 for the instrumental album he did with Chet Atkins when Atkins subsequently introduced him to Glen Campbell. Glen invited him first as a guest and then as a regular for three years on his popular television show, "The Goodtime Hour." That exposure in turn attracted the attention of Burt Reynolds, who auditioned and signed Jerry for the role of Wayne in the film "W. W. and the Dixie Dancekings" in 1973, and the "good ole boy" chemistry between the two led to further parts for Jerry in "Gator" and both "Smokey and the Bandit" movies. In the first Jerry wrote the hit sound track song, "East Bound and Down." He later did the movie "High Ballin'" with Peter Fonda for which he also penned the hit title song. In all he so far has seven movie credits including "Hot Stuff" with Dom DeLuise and Suzanne Pleshette. He also has done a television film "Concrete Cowboys" and a television mini-series with Claude Akins, "Nashville 99."

In addition to his two Grammys, Jerry also has two Country

Music Association Instrumentalist of the Year Awards and twenty-one BMI Awards for both country and pop performances.

He tried five times to complete his high school education, but finally gave up because he kept "just sitting there running guitar licks in my head." After deciding, however, that his "life's work was going to totally revolve around my music," he has undertaken the serious study of music theory.

He met his wife, Priscilla "Prissy" Mitchell, who now is a talented back-up singer, at the age of seventeen when he was doing a one-night stand at Lithia Springs, and they were married by the time he was eighteen. They and their two daughters live in a Georgian Mansion in Nashville and the older daughter, Seidina, has a promising career as a singer in her own right, prompting Jerry to say, "Seidina scares me to death. She's got so much talent — just like her mama."

A laid-back, good-natured wise cracker, Reed takes little other than his music seriously and keeps his professional and private lives strictly separated. His only love besides family and music is fishing, but he makes it emphatically clear that "the only thing I'll not quit doing is playing a guitar."

Atlanta Rhythm Section

ATLANTA RHYTHM SECTION

The Atlanta Rhythm Section was composed of six of the most talented young musicians of their or any other time; they have been molded and merchandised by the genius of songwriter/ producer Buddy Buie.

Though some critics have viewed them as no more than a southern boogie band "with class," they have credentials to prove they collectively can produce the magic their publicity promises of making audiences feel a part of their music. As proof of their magic they performed at the White House and have had the cheering ovation of 61,000-plus fans who packed their celebrated Champagne Jam in 1978.

The New York Times calls the group, which was based at Doraville, Georgia, "the best the South has to offer," but an English critic came closer to their true ranking in pronouncing them "the quintessential American Band."

The Atlanta Rhythm Section was not so much the product of creation as evolution, and if it could be said to have had any starting point, that probably would have to be fixed as the time of migration of Dennis Yost and the Classics IV from Jacksonville to Atlanta because it was from that group that guitarist J. R. Cobb and keyboardist Dean Daughtry came and the Cobb-Buie songwriting team developed.

With Barry Bailey on the lead guitar, Paul Goddard on the bass and Robert Nix on the drums, they first sat as a group in 1970 to back-up Roy Orbison in a recording session; with the addition of lead vocalist Ronnie Hammond, a recording engineer who could also play guitar, keyboard and drums, they established themselves as Atlanta's best and most demanded studio back-up group. At the same time, Buie and engineer Rodney Mills, said to be "one of rock and roll's great natural resources," were developing Studio One as one of the nation's finest recording facilities.

185

Unlike other contemporary groups, ARS shunned gimmicks, antics and flashy costuming to emphasize collective and individual talents in the development of a hybrid brand of rock and roll embracing as much British rock as traditional southern rhythm and blues and incorporating melodic strains missing in the music of other southern bands.

There was a strong emphasis on songs, particularly those written by Cobb and Buie, as Buddy searched for "the perfect sound." These efforts, however, tended to keep them in the studio and to give them a faceless image, and it was not until they "took to the streets" with a series of concerts that their work began to be recognized and their albums to sell well.

Although the Cobb-Buie team has written a number of smash successes for the Classics IV, beginning with "Spooky" in 1968, the Atlanta Rhythm Section did not achieve a hit until its sixth album, "A Rock and Roll Alternative." From this, their top single, "So Into You," skyrocketed to the top and gave the group its first Gold Record in 1977. That fall they attracted 50,000 fans to their Dog Day Rock Fest at Grant Field and, with the help of promoter Alex Cooley, topped that with their record "Champagne Jam" the following year. Also in 1978 Chip Carter invited them to entertain at the birthday party given his father at The White House; the President commented that they had much in common in that his and their critics said they "didn't have a chance when they started."

The tag "Champagne Jam" stuck and has been applied to ARS music since. In 1979 they had another pair of singles, "Do It or Die," and a revival of "Spooky," and issued a double album of their earlier work, including the minor hit "Doraville," written by Buie, Bailey and Nix in 1974. In 1980 their tenth album, "The Boys From Doraville," created a stir with "Cocaine Charlie," "Rough at the Edges," and "Next Year's Rock 'N' Roll" and featured the group's new drummer, Roy Yeager.

Three of the band's six members are from Georgia. Barry Bailey grew up in Decatur and started playing guitar on a twenty-dollar Sears Silverstone when he was twelve. Paul Goddard's musical career started in Rome, Georgia, where he beat the vents of the kitchen stove to get different tunes at the age of four until his parents upgraded him to a ukelele. And Ronnie Hammond is from Macon, where he played drums, guitar and keyboards for The Celtics. Cobb and Nix got their starts with Dennis Yost in

Jacksonville, and Daughtry came from Alabama by way of the Roy Orbison organization.

The catalyst of the organization is Buie, who not only gave the band its song-oriented melodic style but also has produced its quality recordings in his Studio One. It was he who insisted that none of the ARS songs run over four minutes, a restraint not characteristic of other rock groups of any section. As a song-writer he had more than twenty chart records in the Sixties; in addition to the Rhythm Section, he also has worked with stars like Tommy Roe and Bobby Goldsboro. He said he is "unashamed" of his love of commercial music and was in New York City writing it when Atlanta music entrepreneur Bill Lowery lured him south with the publication of "Party Girl." Atlanta and Georgia have been his home ever since.

LITTLE RICHARD
(Richard Perriman)

The life story of Little Richard, the "King of Rock and Roll" from Macon, Georgia, is a true story stranger than fiction. No one in his wildest imagination could dream up a biography which has an abandoned black boy from the Deep South taking the name of the rich Jewish family that adopted him, developing with their help into a musical prodigy who speeded up the rhythm and blues of blacks and turned it into the rock and roll of whites, helping the Beatles get started and teaching Paul McCartney to sing, writing songs for Elvis and becoming an ordained minister in the Seventh Day Adventist Church.

Born December 25, 1935, Richard chose the last name of his Jewish benefactors, who were chastised by their family but were undeterred in bringing him up in the gospel music tradition of his race and in helping him become an accomplished pianist by the time he was in his teens. A devotee of rhythm and blues and the new postwar swing form, boogie-woogie, Richard was determined to have a musical career and went to Atlanta, where he washed dishes at the bus station, wrote songs, won a talent contest and got his first recording contract with Camden when he was sixteen.

He made four recordings in October 1951, including a boogie-woogie number and a "moaning" urban song of his own, and added four more in January 1952. Reissues of these reveal him to have had a strong, clear voice and to be the writer of lyrics that tell a definite story. He spent the next two years playing small black nightclubs in the South, experimenting with what was to become his version of rock and noting as he did that it was whites rather than blacks who responded to his material.

While he was cutting some traditional blues songs for Specialty Records in New Orleans in 1954, the producers heard him play his "Tutti Frutti" during a break and asked him to record it. It sold

188

200,000 copies in the first week and a half and went to the top of the charts at the end of 1955; it stayed there through the spring of 1956 and earned him a Gold Record.

That success thrust him into the national spotlight where his multicolored outfits and pomaded pompadour stunned staid music critics. He kept up a steady string of hits including "Long Tall Sally," "Slippin' and Slidin', ""Rip It Up," "Ready Teddy," "The Girl Can't Help It," "Lucille," "Send Me Some Lovin'," "Jenny, Jenny," "Miss Ann," "Keep A-Knockin'," "Good Golly, Miss Molly," "Lawdy, Miss Clawdy," "Oooh! My Soul," "True, Fine Mama," "Baby Face," and "Kansas City."

Eighteen of his singles had sales in the neighborhood of one million each during the Fifties, and his lifetime total had exceeded 32 million by the end of the Seventies. His songs were recorded by Elvis Presley, Buddy Holly, Tom Jones, Pat Boone and Paul McCartney, each of whom had at least one hit with a Little Richard composition. He also did soundtracks for three movies. His group gave starts to stardom to such greats as Jimi Hendrix, Otis Redding, Joe Tex and Billy Preston.

The course of his life was changed, however, while he was enroute to England, where his music had a major impact. An engine in his plane caught on fire over the ocean, and he promised God to enter the ministry if the plane landed safely. It did and he removed all his rings, threw them into the sea and returned to Alabama to earn a divinity degree and be ordained in the Seventh Day Adventist Church.

But he was lured back into performing in 1963 by invitations from the then relatively unknown Beatles and the Rolling Stones to tour with them and play his music in Europe, where it had remained highly popular. He arranged the Beatles' first recording contract with VJ Records and "taught Paul McCartney that little 'oooouu' that he throws in songs like 'I Saw Her Standing There.' "

He returned to the United States to appear before throngs of young rock fans in places like the Whiskey-a-Go-Go on Sunset Strip and at the famed Coconut Grove. He resumed recording with Okeh Records in 1969 and made the charts with "Poor Dog," "I Need Love" and "Hurry Sundown" as he did with his LP, "The Explosive Little Richard." In 1972 his Reprise album, "King of Rock 'n' Roll" was on the charts for a number of months.

But his later records never sold as well as his early ones, and his popularity during this comeback portion of his career was centered largely in rock-revived concerts which attracted standing-room-only crowds of teenaged rockers who wanted to see and hear the man they had heard about from the Beatles, Stones and Tom Jones.

In the Eighties, Little Richard, who now lives in Riverside, California, returned to his religious fervor and the revival circuit. The one thing that riles him is the claim of others to be the originators of rock and roll. As he stated to the magazine Rolling Stone on that subject:

"Like Ford was the founder of the Ford . . . I'm the founder of rock and roll. You understand me? Which was first named Rhythm and Blues. I speeded it up and they called it Rock and Roll."

Little Richard (Richard Perriman)

TOMMY ROE

The phrases "typical American boy" and "bubble gum music" were the ones most often used to describe Tommy Roe of Atlanta, Georgia, and the songs he wrote and recorded in the 1960's and 70's, but the pop rock tunes turned out by that clean-cut graduate of Brown High School turned into some of the biggest hits of the 1962-72 decade and earned for him the royalties which bought the 30-acre farm near Cumming, Georgia, to which he returned in the early 80's as home base for his hoped-for second career in making movies.

Born May 9, 1942, Thomas David Roe was a contemporary of Atlanta Rock Stars Billy Joe Royal and Joe South. Roe, ironically, was a bigger hit in England than in America and found it necessary to move there to establish his stardom back home.

He developed a fine singing voice, formed his own dance group called the Satins and began writing original compositions for them while he was still in high school. One of those songs done while he was in the 10th grade was "Sheila" which went nowhere on its first recording for Judd Records in 1960, but became a No. 1 hit when picked up and promoted by ABC-Paramount Records two years later. It became an even greater smash when covered later in the decade by the Beatles.

Because his follow-up records did much better in England than in the United States, he left his Georgia job as a General Electric technician and moved there to become one of Europe's top in-person performers and to continue recording for ABC, which issued his "Tommy Roe" and "Something for Everybody" albums in 1963; these also sold far better overseas than in America. His single "Sweet Pea" was one of the top sellers in England in 1966 as were his albums of the same title that year and "Phantasy" in 1967. He also appeared in concert with the Beatles, who admired and played his music.

An invitation to appear on Dick Clark's new ABC-TV rock show, "Where the Action Is," brought him back to America and stimulated his popularity with young rock fans in this country to the point where he accomplished the sensational feat in 1969 of placing four consecutive recordings in the No. 1 spot on the national best-seller lists — re-issues of "Sheila" and "Sweet Pea," "Hooray for Hazel" and "Dizzy," which he wrote and recorded with fellow Atlantan Freddy Weller, whom he met while Freddy was playing as lead guitarist with Paul Revere and the Raiders. All four sold more than one million copies each and earned him Gold Records.

He and Weller scored again in late 1969 with "Jam Up, Jelly Tight" which took its title from an expression his father always used to describe things that were OK. This recording made the Top 10 and Gold Record status in January 1970. His album "Twelve in a Roe" was a best seller for the first six months of that year as was his single "Pearl" during the summer. His single and album "We Can Make Music" were hits in the late 70's, and his single "Stagger Lee" made No. 24 nationally in late 1971. ABC also issued retrospective albums of his songs: "Beginnings," "16 Greatest Hits" and "Greatest Hits," and he added another single "Mean Little Woman" to the charts when he switched to MGM Records in 1972.

During the late 60's Roe had one of the country's most successful nightclub and concert acts. He appeared at Disneyland, the Hollywood Bowl and the Sahara Hotel in Las Vegas and made extensive annual tours of England and Europe. He also was featured in a number of joint concerts with Joe South and Billy Joe Royal, including their SRO performance at the Greek Theater in Los Angeles in the summer of 1970. He was a popular guest star on television and headlined such shows as those of Ed Sullivan, Mike Douglas and Virginia Graham.

Although continuing to write songs and running his total number of tunes to more than 200, he took a break from show business in the late 70's and moved to Malibu, California, to contemplate his future. It was during that time that he was divorced from the girl he married while living in Great Britain. In California he began to think seriously about reviving his original boyhood ambition of making and acting in movies. He tried his hand at acting in little theater in Los Angeles, appeared in a production of "Star Spangled Girl" in Lubbock, Texas, and guest starred in some television sitcoms.

He married French actress Josette Banzet and returned to

192

Georgia in 1982 to live on the farm he had bought in Forsyth County with his earnings from his first hit with "Sheila" and to join producer-director Bill Warren in making the movie "Hopefully Yours" in Cartersville and Athens in which he starred and introduced four of his songs. He also resumed concert engagements and appeared with such other veteran rock stars as Rick Nelson, Chuck Berry and Bo Diddley. He also made plans for further movies.

Roe characterizes his music as country rock and attributes the wholesome image of it and of himself to following the advice of his parents when he first began traveling for concerts as a teenager: "Do the right things and stay away from the bad things."

Tommy Roe

DAVID ROGERS

Atlanta's David Rogers falls into the "almost-but-not-quite" category of country music stardom and is a good example of a fine talent having difficulty breaking out of the herd of aspirants who compete for fame and fortune in the country music industry. His recordings have consistently made the charts since "Forbidden Fruit," his first in 1967 to "Hold Me" in 1983. Some critics have called him country music's "finest ballad singer," but the really big break has eluded him.

Born March 27, 1936, he resisted his father's ambition for him to be a doctor, traded his camera for a guitar, and secretly taught himself to pick while in grade school. He began playing for local clubs in Atlanta when only sixteen. He supported himself selling pots and pans door to door and as a draftsman while developing his style working in Kathleen Jackson's Longhorn and later Egyptian Ballroom nightclubs.

Jackson financed a demo tape that fellow Atlantan Pete Drake sold to Columbia which signed him to a five-year contract. Some of his chart records have been "I'd Be Your Fool Again," "I'm in Love with My Wife," "A World Called You," "I Wake Up in Heaven," "She Don't Make Me Cry," "Ruby, You're Warm," "Need You," "Whispers and Grins." In 1973 "Just Thank Me" made the Top Twenty and in 1974 "Loving You Has Changed My Life" made the Top Ten. His album "Farewell To The Ryman" was well received and his latest is the "Best of David Rogers" by Music Masters.

Pete Drake has been a big influence on this talented stylist who according to Drake "really believes in country music."

BILLY JOE ROYAL

Georgia's Billy Joe Royal left the boondocks of Valdosta, where he was born, for the suburbs of Atlanta in 1951 when he was six years old, but the music of his early years stayed with him, and his recording of "Down in the Boondocks" fourteen years later sold more than 2,000,000 copies. It made him a concert superstar whose performances of music alternatively described as "country-soul" and "country rock" have brought him ovations from stages as diverse as those of the London Palladium, the Greek Theater of Los Angeles and the Flamingo Hotel of Las Vegas.

One of the foremost of the young performers who developed around the songwriting and producing talents of Atlanta's great Joe South, Royal got his start singing "Zippy-dee-doo-dah" for a school PTA meeting shortly after his family moved to Marietta.

After learning to play the guitar and piano first under the influence of traditional country performers and then of major rock artists, he formed his own band to play for dances and parties while attending Marietta High School. Billy Joe and the Corvettes were playing small clubs by the time he graduated and shortly thereafter landed a two-year booking in Savannah.

Out of his friendship with South developed the recording sessions which brought out the smash "Down in the Boondocks" in June 1965 and resulted in a recording contract with Columbia Records which issued an album of the same name that made the charts as did a second LP, "Billy Joe Royal," released in November 1965. Guitarist Freddy Weller who played for Royal's rock version of "Boondocks" also made a hit of it under his own name on the country charts.

His recording successes brought Royal many bookings in major cities throughout the United States and abroad. While in London to do the Palladium, he was invited to a Royal Garden Party, where he was presented to the British monarch, and his appearances at the Flamingo caused The Hollywood Reporter to describe him as potentially rivaling Elvis Presley and Tom Jones as a Las Vegas attraction.

In November 1967, the third and last of his albums produced by South was released. It was called "Hush" and took its name from the title of the wailing hit of the "Billy Joe Royal" album. For his next LP in 1969 he switched to Buddy Buie at Studio One; Buie produced "Cherry Hill" and followed up with another in 1971.

Most of Billy Joe's other singles made the charts, including "I Knew You When" and "I've Got to Be Somebody" in 1965, "Heart's Desire" and "Campfire Girls" in 1966, "Every Night" in 1970 and "Tulsa" in 1971. His relatively low output of recordings in the late 60's and early 70's was due to his heavy schedule of concerts and television appearances, the latter of which included appearances on such shows as those of Barbara McNair, Tom Kennedy and David Frost.

Royal makes his home in Atlanta where he works on his music and pursues his favorite pastime, breeding horses.

196   **Billy Joe Royal**

ROBERT SHAW

The one thing which can be said with certainty about Robert Shaw, the colorful and tempestuous music director and conductor of the Atlanta Symphony Orchestra, is that he provokes strong feelings from admirers and detractors alike, and virtually no one is neutral about him, his credentials or his work. On the one hand, he is widely regarded as the world's greatest living conductor of choral music, and media critics generally write about him in lavish terms sometimes acclaiming him a genius; on the other hand, his singers and musicians complain about his ferocious temper tantrums and his audiences sometimes are turned off by his experimentation with a contemporary repertoire.

But whatever the assessment, none denies that in 16 years at its helm, Shaw has transformed the Atlanta Symphony from a parochial ensemble which was the outgrowth of a youth orchestra sponsored by the Atlanta Music Club and had an annual budget of only $300,000 into a nationally recognized, full-time, professional musical organization of 88 members backed by a 250-voice chorus which has an RCA recording contract, is funded in excess of $6 million a year and can draw SRO audiences from the Kennedy Center to Carnegie Hall and win rave reviews from the toughest critics in New York, Chicago, Boston and Washington, D. C.

Shaw was born in Red Bluff, California, in 1916, the second of five children in the singing family of a minister in the Christian (Disciples of Christ) Church, and he went to Pomona College with the intention of either entering the ministry himself or becoming a teacher for comparative religion. That plan changed, however, when during his junior year in 1937 he met Fred Waring, who came to the campus to make a film with Dick

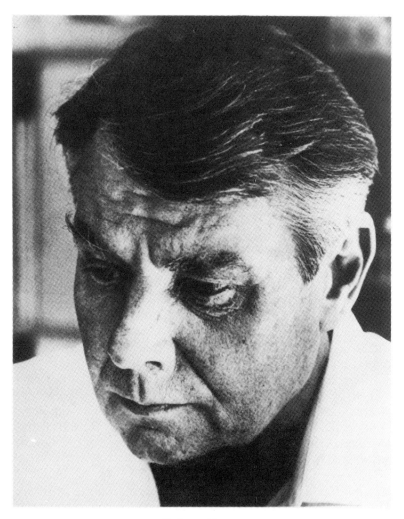

Robert Shaw

Powell was impressed by Shaw's direction of the College Glee Club as a substitute for an ill professor and invited him to come to New York to organize a similar group. Shaw agreed and began the next year. He worked as Waring's right-hand man until 1945 and also formed his own collegiate chorale in 1941. This group brought him to the attention of Arturo Toscanini, who asked him to prepare choruses for all of his major concerts and, despite Shaw's total lack of orchestral experience, invited him to be a guest conductor of the NBC Symphony Orchestra in 1945. That experience prompted Shaw to hire Julius Herford of Indiana University to tutor him in musical analysis and conducting technique in a personal cram course of 40 to 60 hours a week over the next several years; and, about the same time, composer William Schuman, then President of the Julliard School of Music, named him to be director of choral music of that institution despite the fact, as he later told him, that "You were terribly, terribly ignorant." Shaw's fame spread to the point that he soon was leading workshops on choral conducting and guest conducting throughout the nation; and, in 1948, he founded the Robert Shaw Chorale, which basically was a pickup organization built around a nucleus of experienced choral singers with whom he was to achieve fame through concerts, recordings and guest appearances on radio programs and later on television.

His first post as a conductor was with the San Diego Symphony Orchestra from 1953 to 1957, a summer appointment which he combined with six weeks of annual choral workshops at San Diego State College; and in 1956 he became associate conductor of the Cleveland Symphony Orchestra under the legendary George Szell, whose conducting techniques he adopted and adapted and whom he strongly defends against Leonard Bernstein's charge of being the "last of the great tyrants of the podium." His last year there, 1967, overlapped his first as music director in Atlanta, where he succeeded the founding conductor, Henry Sopkin, and diagnosed its problem as "not so much promoting the orchestra as educating the audience."

His leadership in Atlanta, where, contrary to the prevailing trend of jet-setting (or, as Shaw calls them, "suitcase") conductors, he insisted upon being a highly visible resident involved in what he terms the "social matrix," brought a steady upgrading in orchestra personnel, salaries and programming and the recruiting of the best voices from the churches and colleges of the

Atlanta area for his new Atlanta Chorus. However, his edu-
cational efforts, which he described as "marching not just over
the next hill but over the next mountain range," centered on his
attempt to develop a modern repertoire mixing Bartok,
Hindemith and Stravinsky and Beethoven and Berlioz but
proved to be too much for many conservative tastes and brought
him criticism for performances that were said to be too extro-
verted and tedious. Critics likened them to "two tomcats fighting
on a fence at midnight." The resulting decline in season ticket
sales culminated in an effort by the board of directors to fire him
in 1972, but editorial criticism by the Atlanta Newspapers and the
formation of a citizens committee to spur ticket sales by checks
made personally to Shaw brought a reversal of that decision and
an overhaul of the symphony's administrative and business
procedures after Shaw accused the front office personnel of being
"musically and aesthetically unknowledgeable and uncommit-
ted."

Having won that battle and subduing his critics to the degree
that he experienced no further serious problems with his tenure
or programming, Shaw concentrated on building the Orchestra's
national image with wide-ranging concert tours and the development of choral spectaculars which he called "emotional omni-
umgatherum" such as his reading of the requiem masses and the
thundering Beethoven Ninth. The most respected critics applaud
the precision, rhythm and vitality of the Orchestra's performances under his direction. Paul Hume of The Washington Post called his ability for "sustaining the basic rhythmic
foundation" in all of his works "a rare gift" in which other
musicians stand in awe, a capacity sustained by recording
studios which found it necessary to time his takes by a stopwatch
to assure exact and consistent tempo in all parts of each selection.
John von Rhein of The Chicago Tribune and Robert C.
Marsh of The Chicago Sun-Time agreed that the Atlanta
Orchestra under Shaw was better than either the Boston or
Chicago orchestras, and Irving Lowens of The Washington
Star said Shaw's musicians "simply outplayed . . . (and) out-
classed" their Washington counterparts.

Stories of the Shaw temper are legion; from throwing his
glasses across the stage to berating the quality of individual
performances to stalking off the podium when doors are left
open. Some of his most talented singers and musicians have quit
because of his tantrums, one being quoted as saying Shaw gets so

angry he sometimes becomes "totally irrational." He writes open letters of comment and encouragement to his performers, a collection of which comprises a major portion of the recent biography done by Joseph A. Mussulman. He refuses to take bows and leaves the podium with head lowered immediately upon completing his performances. His speech patterns border on stuttering but actually are a stumbling over his words in his enthusiasm to express his thoughts.

He deplores the cynicism he sees creeping into American orchestras and expresses concern about the discouragement that talented musicians are experiencing because of the scarcity of employment opportunities, the uncertainty of regular work and woefully inadequate compensation. He sees the answer to the problem in the creation of what he would call a "Society of Musical Arts" of upwards of 200 musicians and singers in each major metropolitan area which would be involved not only in the city's symphony orchestra but also in opera, chamber music, oratorio and cantata and musical education. He says that was the second of his two goals in coming to Atlanta and emphasizes that he will concentrate on it when he fully realizes the first — "the building of the Atlanta Symphony Orchestra into a great performing insturment" — which he expects to have done by the year 1985 when he will have achieved expansion of the ASO to 103 members for which he has a commitment.

Shaw divorced his first wife, Maxine, in 1970 and started on his second family at the age of 60 with the birth of a son, Thomas Lawton, to his second wife, Carolina, in 1977. Hardy and vigorous at the age of 66 and with three more years to go on his latest contract, Shaw has no thoughts of retirement and feels "like I've got another 30 or 40 years."

201

LYNYRD SKYNYRD

One can get up an argument either way as to whether the southern hard rock booze band Lynyrd Skynyrd was for real or the product of a put-on hype of its charismatic founding leader, singer and songwriter Ronnie Van Zant. But the color and controversy of its performance from its discovery in an Atlanta bar to its demise in a tragic plane crash in Mississippi had a major impact upon both the music and social outlook of disaffected youth of the Seventies, particularly in the South.

The outgrowth of the My Backyard Band started by Van Zant and guitarists Gary Rossington and Allen Collins in Jacksonville, Florida, in 1965, Lynyrd Skynyrd dates from the group's expansion to include bassist Leon Wilkenson, keyboardist Billy Powell, lead guitarist Ed King and drummer Robert Burns, later replaced by Artimus Pyle.

The group's unusual name was the re-spelled name of a high school gym teacher, Leonard Skinerd, who made them get haircuts. Described by critics as looking like "The Furry Freak Brothers doing a guest shot on Star Trek" and notorious for their hard drinking, they gravitated from Florida clubs to Atlanta where their lightning quick three-guitar riffs and their joyously unreconstructed southern style complete with unfurled Confederate Flag attracted a loyal and rowdy following at Funocchio's and the producer Al Kooper who signed them to record for his Sounds of the South Records.

Their records, some of which were done in Buddy Buie's Studio One in Atlanta, became best sellers, "Second Helping" earning a Gold Record, and produced such hit singles as "Sweet Home Alabama," their classic response to the southern slanders of Neil Young, and "Free Bird" a tribute to their idol, Georgia's Duane Allman.

Van Zant's powerful lyrics of social commentary articulated the rage of working-class southern youth about the good life it was impossible for them to achieve but proved to touch responsive chords in disaffected young people throughout the nation.

The band was at the peak of its popularity and in the midst of a nationwide tour which would take it to Honolulu and culminate in a concert at New York's madison Square Garden when the plane in which it was traveling to a date at Baton Rouge, Louisiana, crashed near McComb, Mississippi on October 20, 1977 killing Van Zant, guitarist Steve Gaines, singer Cassie Gaines and an assistant manager. Seriously injured were Rossington, Collins, Wilkenson and Hawkins. Ironically, the group hated to fly and usually traveled in a custom bus, but had to take a charter flight to meet its Louisiana schedule.

The survivors retired the name Lynyrd Skynyrd in tribute to the victims and reconstructed themselves two years later as the Collins-Rossington Band.

THE S. O. S. BAND

The S. O. S. Band is the direct opposite of the signal of distress with which the uninitiated often associate its name.

To the contrary, the initials of the eight-member Atlanta-based music group which specializes in a fresh, space-age mixture of live pop ballads, hard-driving funk and jazz-flavored dance tunes stands for Sounds of Success. These sounds were designed by Los Angeles music producer Sigidi, and they achieved success through the discovery and management of Atlanta promoter Bunnie Jackson Ransom.

S. O. S. had its beginning with Santamonica, the house band of the mid and late Seventies at Atlanta's Regal Room which developed the reputation of having one of the hottest live shows with the performances of singer Mary Davis of Savannah, keyboardist Jason Bryant of Atlanta, drummer James Earl Jones, III, of Philadelphia and saxophonist Billy R. Ellis of Cleveland.

They invited Mrs. Ransom to catch their act, and she was so impressed with the band's penchant for originality that she called their work to the attention of Clarence Avant, President of Tabu Records, who put them under contract and signed Sigidi to shape their sound. He added bassist John Alexander Simpson, III, lead guitarist Bruno W. Speight, saxophonist Willie "Sonny" Killebrew and trumpeter Abdul Raoof and later replaced James as drummer with Jerome Thomas.

The group's first single "Take Your Time (Do It Right)" was a fabulous across-the-board hit. It sold two million records to earn a Platinum Record and achieved simultaneous Number One rankings on the pop, soul and disco charts, the latter for fourteen consecutive weeks in 1980. The S. O. S. album of the same title sold more than 800,000 copies to earn gold status, and on the strength of those successes, the group went on national tour with the Isley Brothers and the Commodores.

As with the first, Tabu joined with CBS Records to issue second and third albums in 1981 and 1982 — the former being

The S. O. S. Band

titled "S. O. S. Band Too" and the latter "S. O. S. Band III."
"Too" produced a hit single in "Do It Now" and received
considerable publicity for its inclusion of the band's own tribute
to Atlanta's murdered and missing children, "Do You Know
Where Your Children Are?" "III" was recorded at Master Sound
and Axis Studios in Atlanta and was produced by Gene Dozier
and Ricky Sylvers with Leon Sylvers serving as executive
producer. It featured songs written by the group's members and
Dozier, who is noted for his horn arrangements on albums by
Shalamar and Dynasty. It headlined the single "High Hopes"
penned by Jimmy Harris and Terry Lewis of the Time. The two
Sylvers joined the venture from production of albums for
Shalamar, the Whispers and Dynasty.

In its later recordings, S. O. S. has expanded from its
typecasting as a dance band and has gotten into message songs
like the one about Atlanta's children and energetic expressions of
the love theme with such Mary Davis tunes as "There Is No
Limit." Under the direction of Sigidi, it has put together a fresh
mid tempo sound balancing a heavy bottom with a sophisticated
string ensemble and strong horn charts on the top, all overlined
with vibrant vocals delivered in a gospel-tinged style.

Its reviews have been almost universally favorable. The Los
Angeles Times calls it "one of the most promising R & B
groups around." The judgment of the Black Music is that S. O. S.
has a "very polished soul sound . . . a mix of disco and soul that's
a sure fire formula." Mexico's Sonida calls their style "the sound
of today."

In 1980 Cash Box Magazine awarded the group five of
its top end-of-the-year awards: Most Promising Group in Black
Singles, Top New Group on Black Singles, Most Promising
Group on Black Albums, Top New Group on Black Albums and
Most Promising Group on Pop Singles.

JOE SOUTH

The one thing on which both the despairing admirers and the admiring detractors of Joe South, Atlanta songwriter and guitarist, agree is that his capacity for putting meaningful words to memorable music was sheer genius.

South started picking out notes on his father's guitar at the age of eight, talked Atlanta Music Producer Bill Lowery into putting him on Radio Station WGST to sing some of his own songs at the age of 12, was playing in Pete Drake's band with Jerry Reed and Ray Stevens and performing on the Georgia Jubilee at the age of 15 and was picking backup for stars like Bob Dylan, Aretha Franklin, Fats Domino, Eddy Arnold, Simon and Garfunkle, Solomon Burke, Conway Twitty, Marty Robbins and Wilson Pickett at the age of 17.

He could have made a career and a fortune as a virtuoso studio guitarist, but he found working under the direction and discipline of others "too frustrating" and signed on as the first artist under contract to Lowery when Bill left his deejay job to set up his own music publishing and recording firm, NRC, in Atlanta. South said he had things he "was really aching to say" and Lowery encouraged him to put them into words and music.

His first song to be recorded was "Let Me Tell You About Love" by Ric Cartey which was released with less than success in 1956 by RCA. The second was a hit he prefers to forget, "The Purple People Eater Meets the Witch Doctor," put out by Lowery in 1958 which made the Top 30 and got South an invitation to appear on Dick Clark's television show. He made it with the first of his message songs with "Concrete Jungle" in the early 60's and moved to Nashville where, although he was in great demand as a session musician, he became discouraged with his inability to sell his own songs and returned to Atlanta and the Lowery fold in 1966.

In two years he wrote and produced a series of hits including "Down In The Boondocks," "I Knew You When," "I Gotta Be

Somebody" and "Hush" for Billy Joe Royal, and "These Are Not My People" for Johnny Rivers.

In 1968 he decided he could do better recording his own materials and signed with Capitol Records which produced a regional hit with "Birds Of A Feather" and a chart album in "Introspect" which contained Joe's classic: "Games People Play," the prospects of which were not realized until other performers began to record it. Capitol reissued the album under the title "Games People Play" in 1969 and both it and the single became Gold Records for South, earning him Grammys for Song of the Year and Best Contemporary Song as well as bringing a third Grammy to Saxaphonist King Curtis for the Best Rhythm and Blues Instrumental Performance. "Games" was recorded by more than 125 other major artists.

South's biggest year was 1971 when his "(I Never Promised You A) Rose Garden" became a No. 1 hit recorded by Lynn Anderson and won a Grammy as the Most Performed Song of that year. It is the best-selling country song in the history of Columbia Records and by 1982 had been played on the air more than two million times to be declared the "biggest country song of the decade" by Billboard Magazine.

He had further successes with his own singles of "Mirror Of Your Mind" and "Walk A Mile In My Shoes." The latter was recorded by Ray Stevens and featured by many major artists, including Harry Belafonte and Lena Horne in their 1970 television special. His album, "Don't It Make You Wanta Go Home," and its title song which was written during a recording session, caught the surge of environmental concern in 1970 and his "So The Seeds Are Growing" moved onto the charts in 1971.

The suicide of his brother, Tommy, started Joe on a downhill slide. He stopped working, and went to Hawaii for two years where, in his words, "Polynesian paralysis set in." When he returned to Atlanta he found musical trends had changed and an album released in 1975 did not do well.

South now 41 years old has devoted himself since 1981 to making a comeback. Lowery produced his first single in six years, "South Georgia Pines," and he received a standing ovation at his first public appearance in that period at Atlanta's Excelsior Mill supper club. His "I Knew You When" recently was revived by Linda Ronstadt and went high in the pop charts.

He was described by Robert Lamb in an Atlanta Weekly profile in 1982 as "the Hamlet of Tin Pan Alley, a sort of melancholy Dane of the Top 40, a man who has thought and thought and thought about things only to find that thought alone can be a never-ending indulgence that slowly paralyzes the will." South who says songwriting is "just my way of communicating," believes that success was his downfall. As he puts it:

"What the books don't tell you is what to do if you do succeed. I was successful at one time and I just stood there and plain didn't know what to do with it. I still don't know. But I'm learning."

Joe South

RAY STEVENS

If there were a decathlon in the music industry, Ray Stevens would have to be a leading contender, because his versatility embraces every aspect of the business.

He not only is a singer, a multi-instrumentalist, a composer, a lyric writer, an arranger and a producer but also is equally at home in the fields of pop, country, blues, rock, ballads, comedy and social commentary as well as having a background in classical piano and music theory.

His roots as a total artist are in the cotton mill town of Clarksdale, Georgia, near Atlanta, where his mother started him at the age of five on the piano with Bach and Chopin. He spent all his spare summer hours around the jukebox at the mill swimming pool and listened to Kitty Wells, Lefty Frizzell, Ernest Tubb and Eddy Arnold, and on Sunday nights he listened to the great radio comedians like Jack Benny and Red Skelton.

When the family moved to Albany when he was ten, his background was broadened by the rhythm and blues of Ray Charles, Fats Domino, the Clovers and the Drifters. As a teenager in Albany, he formed his own dance combo and worked as a disc jockey.

While pursuing a music degree at Georgia State University in Atlanta, he played in a combo with Jerry Reed and Joe South and was introduced by his Sunday school teacher to music publisher Bill Lowery, who recorded his first song, "Silver Bracelet," which became a minor hit on Prep Records. He also changed his name from Harold R. Ragsdale (which Lowery said sounded "like a dog's name") to Ray Stevens by using his middle name and his mother's maiden name.

He developed his flair for comedy by doing bits of his own material during intermissions at the dances played by his combo.

While a junior in college, he recorded for Mercury Records and scored almost immediately with hits like "Jeremiah Peabody's Polyunsaturated, Quick Dissolving, Fast Acting, Pleasant

Tasting, Green and Purple Pills," "Ahab the Arab," and "Harry the Hairy Ape." His first "Sergeant Preston of the Yukon" had to be withdrawn because of the objections of the company holding the rights to the television show of that name.

After working at Monument Records as an A & R man, he overcame the early stereotype of being only a novelty composer with his sardonic and controversial "Mr. Businessman" and followed it with a string of hits: "Along Came Jones," "Gitarzan" and the enduring classic, "Everything Is Beautiful," for which he wrote English lyrics after obtaining rights to the French music. It was recorded with the backings of his daughters' school chorus and earned him the first of his two Grammys and honors from BMI for more than one million performances.

Then came the rollicking antics of Ethel in "The Streak," which sold more than five million records, and his second Grammy for his rendition of "Misty," which was an unplanned, spur-of-the-moment improvisation picked up by an engineer when Ray and his band "were just fooling around in the studio."

"Shriners' Convention," his sensational first record with RCA, sold more than 200,000 copies the first week and made the Top Ten in the second. It is a showcase of Stevens' versatility: he wrote the entire script, did all the background vocals, played most of the instruments, sang all the voices in different octaves and supervised the overdubbing and multi-tracking; thus he not only proved his own genius but also permanently "enshrined" Coy and Bubba into American folklore.

All of his more than twenty albums demonstrate the breadth of his talent and evidence his astounding success in running the gamut between the absurdly humorous and the deadly serious without damaging his credibility as an artist.

His recordings have made him in great demand as a guest performer on television, and he has appeared on the Merv Griffin, Glen Campbell, Dean Martin and Andy Williams Shows and had his own program when Andy signed him as his summer replacement.

He also has experienced tremendous success in television commercials and never misses an opportunity to express his positive feelings about life and his strong belief in America. He attributes most of his success to the perspective he gained in being born and recorded in Georgia and the South and the exposure that the blues and folk music that is integral in the culture of the region gave him. He was inducted into the Georgia Music Hall of Fame in 1981.

Ray lives with his wife, Penny, and their two daughters in the home he designed in Nashville, Tennessee; and besides his family and music, his two great passions in life are football and collecting automobiles.

Ray Stevens

SWANEE RIVER BOYS

The Swanee River Boys broke out of the pack of six gospel quartets operating out of Chattanooga, Tennessee, by adding the "something extra" of diversification of repertoire to include a winning mix of gospel, folk, western, Negro spiritual and popular songs.

With the broadcasting help of the 50,000 watts of Radio Station WSB of Atlanta, Georgia, they became immediately before, during and after World War II one of the most popular precursors of today's male singing groups like the Statler Brothers and the Oak Ridge Boys.

Though they never had a hit recording and they disbanded more than 30 years ago, their group continues to be remembered fondly by everyone old enough to recall its days as a headline act on the pre-and-post war radio network programs, Checkerboard Time sponsored by the Purina Feed Company and the Circle Arrow Show sponsored by the Western Auto Company, and the Thanksgiving of 1947 when they and Atlanta Opera Singer Beverley Wolfe created a national sensation by finishing second and first in that order on the popular NBC radio network talent show, "The Big Break."

Although they prided themselves in sharing equally in both responsibilities and credit, the Swanee River Boys credited Billy Carrier who was born July 16, 1913, near Arthur, Kentucky, and since 1965 has lived in Smyrna, Georgia, with being the moving force in their formation. It was he who teamed with a fellow graduate of the Vaughan School of Music, Stacy Abner of Wedowee, Alabama, to form the quartet known as the Vaughan Four to sing over Radio Station WNOX in Knoxville, Tennessee, and to star with Archie Campbell (now of Hee Haw fame) on that station's Mid-Day Merry-Go-Around in 1938. Over the next two years the group evolved into its permanent composition of Carrier as bartione and guitarist; Merle and Buford Abner as bass and lead singers respectively; and George Hughes of

213

George   Buford   Chuck   Merle   Billy

Swanee River Boys

Texarkana, Arkansas, formerly of the Rangers Quartet and the teacher of Singing Cowboy Jimmy Wakely, as high tenor.

After changing their name at Merle's suggestion to Swanee River Boys, they moved to Chattanooga to broadcast over Radio Station WDOD's Noon Day Frolic and their own 15-minute show sponsored by the patent laxative, Black Draught, and broadcast remote by Nashville's Station WLAC. They incorporated comedy with Buford as their comedian and testimony to their popularity was the overwhelming response of 3,298 requests to an offering of a free photograph of the group. It was there that Carrier met his wife, Willene Daniel, daughter of Gospel Songwriter Roland J. Daniel, who had come from Crossville, Alabama, for an audition.

It became clear, however, that if they were to make it as full-time professional musicians, they would have to break out of the plethora of gospel groups operating out of Chattanooga and they accepted Carrier's suggestion that they broaden their repertoire to include songs of the type made popular by the Sons of the Pioneers, spirituals done in black dialect, traditional folk songs, popular ballads and patriotic and seasonal songs. The approximately 300 songs they committed to memory were almost evenly divided between gospel and secular titles, but the requests they received on tour ran almost two-to-one in favor of the secular material. The meticulous logs kept by Carrier showed they had performed 508 times when they were signed in the spring of 1941 to an exclusive, five-year contract by J. Leonard Reinsch to appear on WSB after the Cox organization brought him from WLS in Chicago to reorganize the country music programming of "The Voice of the South."

At WSB they starred with Hank Penny, Pete Cassell, James and Martha Carson and Billy's younger brother, Fiddler Cotton Carrier, on the Saturday Night Barn Dance and every afternoon on the Little Country Church House. Their most requested song was, "I've Found A Hiding Place" followed closely by "Dese Bones Gwinna Rise Again" and "Carry Me Back To Ol' Virginny," the latter done so convincingly in Negro dialect by Buford that many listeners thought they were black. In late 1941 they were invited to join the transcribed Checkerboard Time and made regular trips to St. Louis, Missiouri, to make those recordings. Their popularity as concert artists skyrocketed and they made more than 1,500 appearances during their time with

WSB which continued until Merle and Buford entered military service in late 1943.

Billy and George tried non-music-related jobs in Louisville, Kentucky, but returned to Atlanta in 1944 to reform the Swanee River Boys with Leroy Abernathy of Canton, Georgia, who later would go on to become a member of the Gospel Music Hall of Fame, and Bill Lyles who later would become a member of the famed Blackwood Brothers Quartet until his tragic death in an airplane crash. Then in 1946, the original group got back together and, after a brief stay with WSB, went to WBT in Charlotte, North Carolina, and then to WLW in Cincinnati where they worked in both radio and television and starred on the Circle Arrow Show until Billy left the group in January 1952 and the remainder disbanded later that year. They made their only recordings during that last year, four sides for MGM while Billy was with the group and 10 sides for King after his departure.

Billy and Willene Carrier had their own Sunday program on Radio Station WPFB in Middletown, Ohio, for 10 years while Billy worked at non-musical jobs; and, after they moved to Smyrna, for three years performed with their son, Larry, on Atlanta Station WYZE every Sunday. All the original group now are retired, Buford Abner living in Indianapolis, Indiana, and Merle Abner and George Hughes residing in their respective hometowns.

THE TAMS

Five young black men with the single ambition to rise out of the Atlanta ghetto into which poverty had them trapped pooled their vocal talents to develop a unique a cappella singing style and their meager financial resources to buy matching multi-colored tam-o'-shanters to top their street attire of T-shirts and jeans in the Fifties to become the acclaimed singing and dancing group called the Tams.

They made musical history in rhythm and blues in the Sixties and in beach music in the Seventies and Eighties. Four of the original members were still going strong when they received the Beach Music of the Decade Award at the first Annual Beach Musical Awards ceremonies held in Myrtle Beach, South Carolina in 1982.

Lead singer Joseph Lee Pope, baritone Charles Walter Pope and tenor Horace (Sonny) Key started singing together in high school. They persuaded bass singer Robert Lee Smith, who collected rents in the boardinghouse where they practiced, and lead singer Floyd Ashton to join them when they decided to form a vocal group to sing for tips and whatever else they could get in small clubs and at private parties around Atlanta.

Because they were averaging only about $1.25 a night when they worked, they decided their act needed some distinction; so they pooled their earnings until they could afford to buy the set of bright, matching tam-o'-shanters which gave them their name.

Two songwriting students at Georgia Tech, Cliff and Ed Thomas, caught one of their acts and persuaded the group to make a demo tape in their dormitory room at Tech. They, in turn, took the tape to Atlanta music producer Bill Lowery. The tape featured three of their original compositions, "It's Alright (You're Just in Love)," and "Disillusioned," and Lowery liked the latter two so much that he and Joe South produced the group's first single of them on the Arlen label. The songs became a local hit, and the Tams followed then with four more singles. Because of the difficulty Ashton had in recording lyrics at the initial session, he was dropped from the group, and Joe Pope became the group's permanent and only lead vocalist until Joseph Jones joined them later.

Believing the group had more than local potential, Lowery called them to the attention of ABC/Paramount Records, which signed them to a long-term contract and made their first single "What Kind of Fool (Do You Think I Am)," which on its release in October 1963 became an instant Number 1 hit.

It was followed by such favorites as "You Lied to Your Daddy," "Silly Little Girl," "I've Been Hurt," "It's Better to Have Loved a Little," "Shelter," "A Little More Soul," "Love, Love, Love" and "Hey Girl, Don't Bother Me." This last song, when later released in England, became a Gold Record on the Probe label and made the Tams even bigger stars there than in the United States (an amazing result considering the tune was written on the spur of a moment to fill an album). Their biggest hit of all came in 1968 with "Be Young, Be Foolish, Be Happy," an original composition by Ray Whitley and J. R. Cobb.

With their new wealth, they bought themselves flamboyant outfits, featuring violet and orange vests, flowered shirts and rainbow bell bottom pants to complement their trademark and hired Albert Cottle, Jr., of the Queen City Gospel Singers to join them a choreographer and additional vocalist. With fancy new steps to match their colorful new costumes, they not only became one of the most popular acts on the R & B circuit where they won favor with the soul audiences but also became favorites on college campuses. Billboard Magazine in 1966-67 listed the group as one of the Top Ten Favorites among college music fans.

Their LP's also did well: "Presenting the Tams" made the Top Ten on the R & B hit lists, and "Hey Girls, Don't Bother Me" and "Time for the Tams" showed on the charts in the sixties. in all, ABC released nineteen singles and five albums, and Lowery did "Best of the Tams" on his 1-2-3 label released by Capitol, which also released a "Tams Medley" single. In 1971 the group's switching to Dunhill Records resulted in the sensational English release of "Hey Girl, Don't Bother Me."

In 1970 the Tams signed a management contract with Carolina Attractions and, under the guidance of Harold Thomas, developed into one of the hottest beach music acts in that medium. As a result they received the top beach music award at the first of the annual presentations in that category in 1982 and they are still going strong in 1983.

The Tams

GID TANNER
and
THE SKILLET LICKERS

When music historians sit down to sort out the what and why of 20th Century American Music, they will have to accord high ranking to the influence of Gid Tanner on all of its forms. Tanner, a Georgia chicken farmer, never in his life fully comprehended the importance of the bridge he and his wild band of musical geniuses known as the Skillet Lickers built between traditional folk and modern popular music.

They not only gave respectability and popularity to what previously had been derided as "hillbilly" music but also served as the initial catalyst in the sweeping electronic evolution which brought this nation's music to the mix of country, jazz, blues and urban pop which gives commonality to American music as we know it today.

Had it not been for the lure of the burgeoning music recording and radio broadcasting industries, James Gideon Tanner probably would have been content to limit his musical activities to occasional forays out of his Walton County farm to joust with the likes of Fiddlin' John Carson, his senior, and Clayton McMichen, his junior, in the fiddling competitions of the time, which he sometimes won and in which he always placed.

But then Frank Walker of Columbia Records invited him at the age of thirty-eight to come to New York to help that company catch up with Okeh Records' highly successful issues of Carson's country recordings. He took with him his blind friend, Riley Puckett, who was to gain fame as the first of the crooners and rhythm guitarists, and on March 7, 1924, they became the first southern rural artists to record for Columbia.

Further at Walker's request, he came home and assembled the Skillet Lickers which, with periodic shifts in membership, was to

Gid Tanner
Courtesy of the Country Music Foundation Library and Media Center

become one of the most highly respected and popular names in the field of string band music. From 1926 until their final disbandment in 1934, they made a phenomenal total of 565 recordings combining hillbilly with popular music including the forever popular "John Henry" and the classic "Down Yonder," which was one of the first records to sell a million copies. They also introduced comedy to the recording industry with their rural skits borrowed from the minstrel show format of humorous dialogue interspersed with snatches from previously recorded songs and instrumentals.

Besides Tanner and Puckett, the Skillet Lickers originally included McMichen and his brother-in-law, Bert Layne, as fiddler and Fate Norris on the banjo and the harmonica. Layne was replaced by McMichen's brilliant young protege, Lowe Stokes, from Rome, Georgia, whose contest with Carson for the Fiddlin' Championship was the subject of Stephen Vincent Benet's "The Mountain Whippoorwill." Tanner's younger brother, Arthur, sat in on earlier sessions, and his son, Gordon, played on the last one in 1934. Also with the group at one time or another were Ted Hawkins on the fiddle and mandolin and Mike Whitten and Hoke Rice on the guitar.

Because of personal predilections, conflicts, and musical preferences, most of these men recorded and performed from time to time with different groups of their own or others and sometimes under different names. The differences revolved mainly around the tendency of McMichen to veer off onto progressive and experimental styles as opposed to the conservatism of Norris and the middle-of-the-road traditional inclination of Gid Tanner.

Tanner had an intuitive sense of what would please the public, and he remained the undisputed leader and pace setter of the group because of his capacity to warm up audiences together with his recognition that the success of the band lay in featuring Puckett's singing.

The recordings from the first session in April 1926 were labeled "Gid Tanner and his Skillet Lickers, with Riley Puckett," but because of McMichen's objections based on the argument that the original "Lick the Skillet Band" had been his, all subsequent records added "and Clayton McMichen." For many years it was believed the band featured a two-fiddle lead, but research has demonstrated that it was a three-fiddle band from the beginning, with McMichen and Tanner playing the high parts while Stokes added the baritone. The confusion arose from the fact that Tanner was kept off mike and Stokes was required to play with a mute at McMichen's insistence to make certain he was heard.

All critics agree, however, that it was Stokes' brilliant fiddle added to Puckett's strong contrapuntal bass runs on the guitar that gave the Skillet Lickers the exciting, wild sound that set them apart as a string band and that it was their incorporation of elements which we know today as jazz, bluegrass, western swing and rhythm and blues that gave their music broad appeal.

Tragedy in the form of an accident which cost Stokes his right hand and the Depression which left the people with no money to spend for music in any form forced the initial dissolution of the band in 1931. Tanner, who never ceased being a farmer first and a musician second, went back to his chicken farm and also worked at several radio stations. He and McMichen never got back together, but he did reassemble the band in March 1934 to record twenty-four sides for RCA Victor. The band comprised of Tanner and his son, Gordon, on the fiddles, Puckett on the guitar and Hawkins on the mandolin turned out a sound that was different with the mandolin carrying the musical lead and Gid Tanner singing the vocal lead. The numbers were almost entirely traditional dance tunes, fiddle songs and instrumentals with several duets with Tanner and Puckett.

Gid Tanner continued to make appearances and to compete in fiddling contests until his death in 1960. He won his last Old Time Fiddler's Contest at the age of seventy-one in 1955. He had been married twice and had five sons. Gordon, who followed in his footsteps, and died in 1982 while attending an Old Time Music Festival in Delaware.

FREDDY WELLER

"Prodigy"is the word often used to describe Atlanta's multi-talented Freddy Weller. His incomparable career, which began when he was fifteen, spanned the spectrum from lead guitarist with the hit-parading rock group Paul Revere and the Raiders to writer and recorder of a string of the greatest country hits of the late 60's and 70's.

Born September 9, 1947, Weller came to the attention of Joe South, Ray Stevens and their mentor, Bill Lowery, when he won the Georgia Jubilee Talent Contest in East Point at the age of fifteen. By the time he graduated from high school, he was playing bass and rhythm guitar for South's band, the Believers. He backed South on his great popular hit "Games People Play" and Billy Joe Royal on his million-seller "Down in the Boondocks." While Weller was sharing a bill in Birmingham, Alabama, with the teenage Revere organization, Revere was so impressed that he invited young Weller to join his group and, after his refusal, persisted with offers until he finally found them impossible to refuse.

Freddy confounded Raider fans with the country numbers he interspersed with their rock renditions and occupied his spare time on the road teaming with Tommy Roe to write a series of "bubble gum" hits which included million sellers "Dizzy" in 1968 and "Jam Up and Jelly Tight" in 1969. When Weller made an appearance on the Ed Sullivan Show, the exposure boosted Weller's popularity and his fame took off in inverse proportion to the declining fortunes of the Raiders. Revere, sensing Weller's great country potential, persuaded Columbia Records to put him under contract.

Beginning with his country version of "Games People Play," which went to number one in 1968, Weller scored with successive hits with "Down in the Boondocks," "The Promised Land," "Indian Lake," and "Another Night of Love" as well as smash albums bearing the first three titles. Although he caught some flack from a few country fans because of his long hair, the criticism dissipated with the rise of older contemporaries like Kris Kristofferson and Waylon Jennings. He had other chart records with "These Are Not My People," "Listen to the Young Folks," "Ballad of a Hillbilly Singer," "The Perfect Stranger," "She Loves Me Right Out of My Mind," "The Roadmaster," "I've Just Got to Know," "Sexy Lady," "You're Not Getting Older," "Liquor, Love and Life," and others.

He also had his own songs recorded not only by his old buddies, Joe South, Tommy Roe, Billy Joe Royal, and Paul Revere but also by such superstars as George Jones, Barbara Mandrell, Del Reeves, Judy Miller and Hugo Montenegro. He operates his own music publishing company, Young World Music, in Atlanta.

Weller finds no contradiction or conflict between his country roots and early rock inclinations. He is proud of his role in the development of the contemporary country sound. His idols are George Jones and Merle Haggard, and he insists that "home is where the heart is and my heart has always been set on becoming a country music recording artist."

225   **Freddy Weller**

HEDY WEST

Hedy West, born April 6, 1938, in Cartersville, Georgia, is a folk singer in the classic tradition who, though now living in London, is better known in Europe than in her native Georgia.

She sings the traditional songs of Appalachia exactly as they were handed down for generations from her great grandparents, Asberry Kimsey and Talitha Prudence Sparks Mulkey of Gilmer County, Georgia, and as they were taught to her by her banjo-playing grandmother, Lillie Mulkey West, and her poet father, Don West, who lived for many years in Pickens and Union Counties in North Georgia and who now is Founder and Director of the Appalachian Folklife Center in Pikestem, West Virginia.

Hedy's musical education was a melange of the classical piano lessons insisted upon by her parents and the self-taught banjo picking of the songs learned from her grandmother. Her local fame as a singer of old songs led to applause as a singer at a festival in Boone, North Carolina, in 1956 and the winning of first prize in a folk song contest in Nashville, Tennessee, two years later.

She pursued her education in symphonic music at Columbia University while also performing the traditional songs of her family in coffee houses from New York to Chicago and, by invitation of Sing Out! Magazine, at Carnegie Hall. By the mid 1960's she had performed at most major folk festivals in the United States, recorded two albums of her songs for Vanguard Records, composed music to go with her father's poem "Anger to the Land," and joined Bobby Bare and Charlie Williams in writing the 1963 country hit recorded by Bare, "500 Miles Away from Home."

Disillusioned by American politics, the nuclear arms race and the Vietnam war, she moved to London at the end of the 60's and recorded extensively and performed widely throughout Europe. By the end of the 70's only one of her albums, "Old Times and Hard Times" on the Folk-Legacy label, remained in general distribution in the United States. In the accompanying notes for that LP, A. L. Lloyd calls Hedy "among the best women singers in the American folksong revival" and notes that she is one of the few performers belonging to "that happy band who are entirely at home in either . . . the world of fine arts or that of folk arts." He points out that she performs the repertoire of her family songs in a straightforward, unpretentious manner and is "not the kind of singer who acts the 'country-cousin' and wears a cotton bonnet and makes a nasal caricature of her 'down-home' vocal style just to charm city audiences."

Her uncle, Harold West, was Editor and Publisher of The Towns County Herald and North Georgia News in Union County for many years prior to his death, and her aunt continues to publish both.

CHUCK WILLIS

The legend is larger than the life of Chuck Willis, the "King of the Stroll," who was born and died in Atlanta and whose death at the age of thirty cost him the personal fame later enjoyed by his successors like James Brown and Otis Redding.

But the supreme irony of his brief career as one of the most influential black rhythm and blues singers was that the song "What Am I Living For?" became a best seller one month after his death and earned him a posthumous Gold Record.

He was born January 31, 1928, in what was described as a "ghetto situation," began singing in neighborhood joints at the age of eighteen, became vocalist for Red McAllister's band in 1950 and, under the management of Zenas "Daddy" Sears, the white guru of Atlanta R & B, signed a contract in 1951 to record for Okeh the "race" label of Columbia Records.

His first success came with the double-sided hit, "Caledonia" and "My Story," in October 1952, followed by other southern best sellers like "Don't Deceive Me" and "I Feel So Bad" in 1953 and 1954. He did not achieve national fame, however, until Sears arranged a new contract with Atlantic Records, where Willis scored with "Juanita" and "It's Too Late" in 1956 and followed with the biggie, "C. C. Rider," which went pop and established him as a major rock and roll artist with both white and black audiences. He followed with another hit, "Betty and Dupree."

Chuck went on the road wearing a turban and doing the dance that dubbed him the "King of the Stroll" and sometimes the "Sheik of the Shake"; but illness overtook him and he died in the hospital on April 10, 1958, from what Sears said were complications from stomach ulcer and his failure to follow doctor's orders. Others claim, however, that he died in an automobile accident, but recording industry rumors said that death was the result of a brain tumor and that the reason he wore a turban was to hide the scars of brain surgery.

In addition to the huge success of "What Am I Living For?"

which became Number One on the American R & B charts and was a hit in England, several other fine Willis blues performances turned up in the Atlantic label, and no one ever was able to trace the date and place of their production, although they generally are attributed to the session at which he collapsed. In later years, Columbia reissued much of the material on an Epic album, and most of the songs he wrote that became hits are included in a current Atco album.

Sears, who regarded Willis as a better songwriter than a performer, agrees with the assessment of Willis' potential for stardom had he lived but points out his life was not as glamorous as legend would have it.

Zenas Sears

DENNIS YOST
and
THE CLASSICS IV

Dennis Yost was born in Detroit, Michigan, and grew up and learned music in Jacksonville, Florida, but it was in Atlanta, Georgia, that he and his group achieved fame as Dennis Yost and the Classics IV.

During a five-year period beginning in 1968, they had thirteen consecutive chart singles, including three which reached Number Two nationally, and an album that remained in the Top Fifty for twenty weeks.

With Yost's vocals, coupled with the sensational songwriting and production talents of J. R. Cobb and Buddy Buie, who went on to found the even more successful Atlanta Rhythm Section, the group was one of the most popular soft-rock sounds of the late Sixties and was featured on most major television network shows. It had several highly acclaimed European tours before Yost went back to Florida to go into business.

As lead singer and drummer and with his high school classmate, Wally Eaton, as rhythm guitarist and songwriter, Yost established his rock group in Jacksonville in 1962 and switched to Atlanta to take advantage of the growing popular recording business there. By 1967 with Cobb on lead guitar, they gained a club following and recorded the Cobb-Buie classic "Spooky," which scored hits both as a single and as an album of the same title the following year.

Although Cobb and Buie left to pursue their individual and collective careers, they continued to write and produce for the group which was billed as "Dennis Yost and the Classics IV" after realignment with the singing of Auburn Burrell as guitarist and Dean Daughtry as keyboardist. Their "Spooky," which became the Number One hit of 1968, sold more than two million copies

Dennis Yost and the Classics IV

and was followed by two more Cobb-Buie best sellers, "Traces" and "Every Day With You, Girl."

From 1968 to 1970, the group was one of the hottest and most sought after in the country; they appeared on American Bandstand and the Tonight, David Frost, and Mike Douglas Shows and were honored by a party given by Nancy Sinatra.

In 1970 they changed from the Imperial to the Liberty/VA and then to MGM Record labels and, in a two-year period, had hit singles with "The Funniest Thing," "Midnight." "Where Did All the Good Times Go," "It's Time for Love" and "What Am I Crying For" as well as top albums titled "Traces" and "Golden Greats — Vol. 1."

Tiring of the pressures, depressed by the departure of talented associates to the Cobb-Buie organization, and searching for a less complicated lifestyle, Yost disbanded the group in 1972 and returned to Florida to indulge his passion for fishing and to go into the retail floor covering business.

However, by 1977 he decided singing was in his blood and organized another group to play the Holiday Inn circuit, to cut albums of "oldies" for television marketing and to try a comeback with Robox Records for which he issued the album "Going Through the Motions" featuring the title song by Hal Bynum, the co-author of "Lucille," in May 1981. In his search for a second musical career as a solo artist, he billed himself as "The Classic One."

AND MANY MORE . . .
(Over 100 brief sketches of other artists)

The overriding dilemma of anyone undertaking to list the greats in any field of human endeavor is not who to include but who one may omit. There are always more success stories than can be told within the limits of a single printed volume. This is very true in the field of music. Determining which of the many talents whose contributions to Georgia's musical greatness should have sections in this book was particularly difficult. I am acutely conscious of this by virtue of my experience with a previous book, Great Georgians, where both my selections and omissions were disputed by some. Therefore, I apologize in advance to all those whose particular favorites have not been included or were not treated in depth.

In this chapter I want to list those worthy of inclusion on any list of Georgia musicians and to whom I would have devoted more detailed sketches had space and time permitted. But, before doing that, there are several special Georgians of whom I wish to make separate mention because, while not musicians themselves, their many contributions to Georgia Music are deserving of particular recognition:

Russ DeVault and **Bill King,** two very talented writers with the Atlanta Newspapers, have reported in depth on the Georgia music scene for many years. (This writer wishes he had their knowledge and insight into the business, not to mention their ability to put it into words.)

J. Garland Pembroke (Jack Tarver, Jr.) with his pen has opened the door of country music to many who would not otherwise have read about it.

Lee Walburn, present editor of Atlanta Weekly, has written some of the best country music columns I've ever read.

Billy Dilworth, Athens newspaper columnist, who for more than 20 years has emceed a country music show on radio station WLET in Toccoa, Georgia, and consistently has won awards as one of the nation's top country disc jockeys.

Paul Hemphill, Atlanta author, whose book, "The Nashville Sound" was one of the first books on country music.

Don Rhodes, music columnist and reporter, of Augusta whose "Ramblin' Rhodes" column appears regularly in the newspapers of Augusta, Savannah, Athens and Jacksonville, Florida, whose recent book, "Down Country Roads with Ramblin' Rhodes" has been widely acclaimed and who is a nationally recognized authority on blue-grass and country music.

The late **Jim Wilder** of Marietta, the owner until his death in 1982 of country music station WBIE in Marietta, was beloved by all country music artists for his continuing support of the business and for his understanding and generosity in encouraging and giving free air time to new songwriters and performers.

In making the above and following listing, I acknowledge that undoubtedly there are many others who should be on the lists and I urge readers to let me know of those omissions so those names can be added in the printing of future editions.

Alphabetically, some very notable Georgia artists are:

Bobby and Mac Atcheson of Atlanta, fiddle and steel guitar duo who played for WSB on both Radio Barn Dance and with the WSB-TV Peachtree Cowboys and subsequently worked as scenic designer and floor manager respectively for WSB-TV.

Dorothy Alexander, Georgia's grand dame of the dance world, was the founder of the Atlanta Ballet, the oldest continuous dance company in America.

Atlanta, a country music group that has scored early success with two Top 20 hits, was among those nominated by the Country Music Association in 1984 for Group of the Year.

Christian Badea, 35 year old Romanian, is the musical director of the Savannah Symphony.

Doc and Lucy Barnes of Athens exemplify the vitality of black sacred singing in the South and have performed for decades throughout the area. Doc has made and can make music from a "quill" that was an instrument of slaves on the antebellum plantations. It is a reed, notched and tuned with wood plugs.

Marcus Bartlett of Atlanta, retired Cox Broadcasting Company executive who was staff pianist, organist and member of the staff orchestra of radio station WSB, now also retired from a second career as professor of broadcast journalism at the University of Georgia Henry W. Grady School of Journalism and Mass Communication.

Debbie Bass, "Little Miss Dynamite" has been a local star in Atlanta night clubs for a long time.

Danny Beard of Atlanta, co-owner with British partner Peter Dyer of independent Atlanta recording label, DB Records, specializing in recording the "Athens Sound" of bands like Pylon, B-52's, Love Tractors and Swimming Pool Q's.

Mandy Beason of Atlanta, pop singing star of musical revues at The Upstairs, the cabaret adjunct to Atlanta's famed Gene and Gabe's Restaurant.

Jackey Beavers of Cartersville, songwriter for Motown Records and writer of the Supreme's hit, "Some Day, We'll Be Together," now executive assistant to Governor Joe Frank Harris.

William Bell, based in Atlanta, who penned the classic "Born Under a Bad Sign" and who in the 1960's worked with all the great blues singers out of Memphis. Artists like Rod Stewart, Lou Rawls and Albert King have recorded his tunes.

Buddy Blackmon of Washington, former player in the bluegrass group, Rocky Mountain Strings, and now leader of Jerry Reed's Band.

Roger Boling of Dillard, major country songwriter who wrote "Lucille," "The Coward of the County," "Blanket on the Ground," and other hits before his death in 1983.

Brenda Boozer, as famous in Europe as she is in her native Atlanta, debuted with the Metropolitan Opera Company in 1979. She is a mezzo-soprano and in her mid 30's. Her parents are with Emory University and she is married to comedian Robert Klein.

Steve Brantley of Augusta, well-known Nashville session musician and backup player for Barbara Mandrell and Ronnie Milsap.

Helen Bickers, young Atlanta soprano and finalist in Metropolitan Opera auditions, sang in "Carmen" with the Summer Opera Theater Company in Washington, D. C.

B-52's, Athens rock 'n' roll dance group which recorded the single "Rock Lobster" with DB Records of Atlanta which led to a major recording contract with Warner Brothers Records.

The Blue Sky Boys, Earl and Bill Bolick, with their haunting and unique harmony, although not from Georgia, appeared all over Georgia and recorded for Bluebird, the early Victor label.

Catherine Boswell was a blues singer and recording artist of note in the 20's and 30's in Atlanta. She was another popular WSB star.

W. Gary Bruce, of Trion, at 85 years of age, was invited to pick old timey banjo at the Smithsonian Festival of American Folklife in Washington, D. C. He also did a little ballad singing, told a few tall tales, recited a few bawdy toasts learned from his Scottish and Irish ancestors.

Uze Brown is a member of the Morehouse College faculty who is determined to show that a black male can become established in opera. He has been a frequent soloist with the Atlanta Symphony and has arranged spirituals for renowned soprano Jessye Norman, already profiled in this book.

Calhoun Musicland: Incorporated in December, 1981. First show was April 1982, with Ronnie Milsap. The founders and current owners are Haley Stephens, Greg Weaver, Roger Rigney and Sam Moss.

Bill Carlisle is a well known Opry star who played in his early years in Atlanta and on WSB.

Pete Cassell was an early Jim Reeves type who sang and performed on WSB radio and was very popular throughout the South.

Cedar Hill is an Atlanta based bluegrass group that won the McIntosh Country Music Award in 1981. An album "Ruff 'n Ready" did well.

Lew Childre was a popular performer on Atlanta radio during the 1930's and 40's.

Wayne Cochran, white rock and soul singer who lived in various parts of Middle and South Georgia before hitting it big on the Las Vegas circuit with his group, the C. C. Riders, now a born-again Christian who gives testimony on television programs.

Grady and Hazel Cole were Atlanta recording stars in the 1930's and 40's. Grady was also a successful song writer, his best known song being the classic "Tramp on the Street."

Cousin Emmy was one of the first female country music artists to have her own band. She had a national reputation, appeared in some western movies and was on WSB in the late 30's and 40s. First brought the song "Ruby" to national attention.

Crossroads, a leading Augusta rock band of the mid-70's which featured Robbie Ducey who now owns and manages his own recording studio in Evans, Georgia; Jimmy Burch who is now Chief Engineer of the Acuff-Rose organization in Nashville, Tennessee; and the late Tommy Witcher who also founded the "Georgia Prophets."

Crystal Pistol, the musical theater at the Six Flags Over Georgia theme park on the Chattahoochee River outside Atlanta which specializes in the discovery and development of young talent, John Schneider being one of its most prominent alumni.

Cullowhee, an Atlanta-based, North Carolina-bred band has entertained Atlanta audiences five nights a week, 50 weeks a year, hoping to become another "Alabama."

Paul Davis is from Mississippi but has made Atlanta his home for several years. Singer, songwriter, key boardest, and co-producer with Ed Seay, he has many pop hits like "I Go Crazy," "Cool Night," "Sweet Life" and "65 Love Affair." He rarely tours, doesn't record too often and loves to fish at Lake Lanier but his talent is recognized universally. In 1984, he was named male vocalist at the first Atlanta Music Awards.

Bruce Dees of Augusta, well-known Nashville session musician and backup player for Barbara Mandrell and Ronnie Milsap.

Mike Dekel, recognized as "Songwriter of the Year" in Atlanta in 1983, wrote "Scarlet Fever" for Kenny Rogers.

John Dilleshaw recorded on the early Okeh label and was a popular guitarist and performer on WSB in the 1920's and 30's.

Joey Douglas of Douglasville, a singer who was born Joanne Blodgett who has been successful as a club singer in Atlanta, Las Vegas and on the West Coast with a crossover sound combining pop, country and rock.

Ray Eberly, one of the top male vocalists of the "Big Band" era lived in Georgia after his retirement and was buried here after his recent death.

Phil and Nancy Erickson are the founders of the Wits End Players and have created some of the zaniest satire, songs and skits found anywhere. They heard Georgia singing and have kept Georgia laughing for 25 years.

Leon Everette, who at one time lived in Oglethorpe County, was nominated for a Grammy for his "The World's Greatest Star Has Gone Home," and is the star of Orlando records with such hits as "Giving Up Easy," "Don't Feel Like the Lone Ranger," and "Over."

Betty Fisher and her Dixie Bluegrass Band perform at bluegrass festivals across the country.

Jim Fogelsong, president of MCA Records who played guitar in Augusta's Broad Street USO while stationed at Fort Gordon and who signed Terri Gibbs to her MCA recording contract.

Jerry Foster, singer and award-winning country music songwriter who first performed on Station WSAV-TV and at the Bamboo Ranch in Savannah while stationed with the Marine Corps at Paris Island, South Carolina. He went on to write hits like "When You Say Love" for Sonny and Cher, "Would You Take Another Chance On Me" for Jerry Lee Lewis and "The Easy Part's Over" for Charley Pride.

Kelly Foxton of Athens, country singer who was born Joyce Sanders and became star baton twirler for Georgia Tech under the name of Dixie Lee before becoming the singing partner of country music great Hank Snow for four years. Besides the Opry, she has appeared on "Hee Haw" and "Nashville Now."

The Eller Brothers, Lawrence and Vaughn, with their partner on the fiddle, **Ross Brown,** live in Towns County but have taken their traditional Appalachian music repertoire of 200 songs to the Smithsonian in Washington, D. C., and the Edinburgh international Festival in Scotland.

Franklin Music Park in west Georgia, owned and operated by **Hugh Gosdin,** has brought mainly country music to thousands of listeners but also has had Fats Domino as a performer.

"Georgia," a Gainesville-based group, was voted in 1984 the "Most Promising Male Group of the Year" by the Southern Gospel Music Association. Members include **Mike Davis, Terry Dale, Lee Burke and Phil Satterfield.**

The **Georgia Mountain Fair** has for more than 30 years provided excellent country music in Hiawassee. With **Fiddlin' Howard Cummingham** in charge, the music started with local musicians under a tree on a hill, then proceeded to the high school auditorium, next, to a big tent and now in the comfortable million-dollar Robert Anderson Music Hall on Lake Chatuge.

Pop Eckler and The Younguns was a big star in Georgia as a member of WSB's Cross Roads Follies. His most popular recording was "Money, Marbles and Chalk."

Edwin Gerschefski, a noted composer and performer, is a professor of music at the University of Georgia.

Warren Gowers of Augusta, well-known Nashville session

musician, member of Terri Gibbs' original trio and backup player for Barbara Mandrell and Ronnie Milsap.

Amy Grant, fastest-selling artist of contemporary Christian music, was born in Augusta, Georgia, and at the age of 22 in 1983 was named the Gospel Artist of the Year by the Gospel Music Association and presented the Dove Award for her "Age to Age" as the Best Contemporary Gospel Album of the Year.

A. A. "Ahaz" Gray was a legendary fiddler who appeared on WSB Radio and Okeh Records. Between 1919 and 1938, he won the Georgia fiddling championship eight times.

Sheila Waters Greene of Macon is not only the wife of Senator Richard Greene, the long time chairman of the Senate Music Industry Committee, but is also a very talented singer.

Cortez Greer of Augusta, who rose from baggage handler for Delta Air Lines to be a star rock and soul singer known as "Tez" before his accidental death from carbon monoxide poisoning in 1976.

Conner Hall was born in South Carolina but joined the great Georgia gospel group, the LeFevres in 1943. He also was an original member and manager of another great Georgia group, the Homeland Harmony Quartet. He was inducted into the Gospel Hall of Fame in 1979.

Theresa Hamm, only twenty, but already the Conyers resident has been awarded "Most Promising Young Singer" at the Metropolitan Operal Southeastern Regional Auditions in 1983.

Roland Hayes was a pioneer black performer in classical music. He was the first black to sing in many theatres and concert halls throughout the United States and Europe in 1917-20. Hayes was born in the Flatwoods (now Curryville), a small community in Gordon County in 1887.

Yvonne Hodges of Metter, backup singer for Lynn Anderson, Janie Fricke and Spanish Singer Clay Corelli who does singing commercials for United Airlines.

Hugh Hodgson founded the University of Georgia Music Department and was its chairman for many years. He composed the "Bulldog Fight Song" but he did much more than that for a generation of students who had their musical horizons broadened by this remarkable man who died in 1969. He was a pianist, an organist and an arranger. He had a talent for explaining music to those with no previous understanding. Ralph McGill called him "Johnny Appleseed of Music in Georgia."

Holiday Beach Opry House: Ribbon-cutting ceremony for opening was May, 1978. Elijah Walden and Allen Paul were original owners; Paul is now sole owner. They first built an open-air structure and it was later enclosed in an air-conditioned building.

Randy Howard is a musician from Milledgeville who has taken top honors throughout the South in bluegrass festival contests.

Dean Hudson of Atlanta, leader of one of the larger and better known big bands of the pre-and post-World War II era who still is popular on the college, country club and convention dance circuits.

Larry Hudson, country singer born in Hawkinsville and raised in Unadilla whose song, "Just Out Of Reach," recorded with Willie Nelson in the Capricorn Studio in Macon became No. 32 on the national lists and whose subsequent "Loving You In a Natural High" hit No. 28, "I Can't Cheat" No. 30 and "I'm Still In Love With You" charted.

Neal James, a native of Commerce and a favorite around Athens for years, has had a nationally recognized album "Living and Loving" and a hit single "Hurricane Shoals."

Hugh Jarrett, the disc jockey on many stations over the years, was with the excellent gospel group, the Jordanaires, who also provided the backup on many of the Elvis Presley recordings.

John Jarrod who left Gainesville a few years ago to write songs for Louise Mandrell, Don Williams and other Nashville artists. His song for Williams, "Nobody But You" went to No. 5 in the nation.

Sammy Johns, another very successful member of the Lowery Group, had a hit record "Chevy Van" in 1974 selling close to 3 million copies and going to No. 2 in the national charts. "Early Morning Love" and "Rag Doll" were mid-chart singles. With Elektra Records, his singles "Common Man" and "Love Me Off the Road" garnered considerable pop and country air play. The former later became a smash for John Conlee. He is presently recording for Southern Tracks.

Bobby Johnson and the Swinging Gentlemen for years entertained audiences all over Georgia, particularly at the WPLO Shower of Start programs and the Georgia Mountain Fair in Hiawassee. Regulars included **Jerry Hall, Houston and James Childers.**

240

Doug Johnson is a promising young song writer with the Lowery organization from Swainsboro. He wrote the hit song, "Simple Little Words" for Christy Lane.

Archie Jordan, country song writer who was born in Augusta and lived eight years in Metter, wrote the hits "What A Difference You Made In My Life" and "Let's Take The Long Way Around The World" for Ronnie Milsap, "Drifter" for Sylvia and "It's All I Can Do" for Anne Murray.

Carole Joyner of Decatur, composer with Ric Carty of the hit song, "Young Love," which has sold more than 15 million copies and been smash hits for four artists — Sonny James, Tab Hunter, Lesley Gore and Donny Osmond.

Harpo Kidwell of Atlanta was the harmonica-playing "Kentucky Colonel" on the original Barn Dance of Atlanta's Radio Station WSB.

Chick Kimball of Atlanta was a star of the original Barn Dance on Atlanta's Radio Station WSB and was particularly known for his Wildroot Hair Tonic commercials.

Ron Kimball has had a large following for many years playing his special brand of country-rock in the metro area.

Lanierland started in 1971 in an old circus tent which was used for three years until a tornado destroyed it and the present building was erected. In 1971, the original owners were C. E. Samples and "Shorty" Hamby. The owners now are Tommy Bagwell, C. E. Samples, Leon Jones and Charles Hailey and Hailey is also the Manager. They are in their 14th season in 1984.

Chuck Leavell, previously mentioned as a key member of the Allman Brothers Band, has also worked with Kitty Wells, the Rolling Stones, the Marshall Tucker Band and others.

Sea Level, a six-man aggregation featuring many of Macon's finest had five excellent albums.

Sonny Limbo of Atlanta who also has a home in London is a song writer and record producer who co-wrote the Gladys Knight hit, "Midnight Train To Georgia" with Jim Weatherly and the Bertie Higgins' hit, "Key Largo," with Higgins. Before coming to Atlanta he worked with Sun Records in Memphis where he helped produce recordings by Elvis Presley, Jerry Lee Lewis and Carl Perkins and then with Fame Studios in Muscle Shoals, Alabama, where he worked with Rick Hall and became executive president of that firm.

Mosie Lister, who now lives in Tampa, Florida, worked in the 1940's and 50's in Georgia and in 1976 was elected to the Gospel Music Hall of Fame. He is not related to Hovie, another famous name in gospel music, but did work some with the Statesmen. He wrote many songs, including "How Long Has It Been?" "Then I Met the Master," and "Till the Storm Passes By," and was involved in the music publishing business.

Charles Mann, singer, actor and composer, who has had his work recorded by B. B. King, Roberta Flack, Donny Hataway and others. He had made television appearances on "Soul Train" and "The Mike Douglas Show." He directed the music for the Atlanta production of "The Wiz" and has composed a musical entitled "Savannah."

Melanie Massell of Atlanta, daughter of former Atlanta Mayor Sam Massell, who is a nightclub singer in the modes of Bette Midler, Patsy Cline and Pat Benetar.

Anita Sorralls Wheeler Mathis was Georgia fiddler champion in 1934, the first and, I believe, only woman to ever win that honor. Her artistry was recognized throughout the South in the 1930's.

Tim McCabe, one of the leaders in the music industry in Georgia, makes money writing commercial jingles for leading businesses but is best know for his sensitive "Springtime in Atlanta" and other songs about Georgia and our people and places.

Thelma "Butterfly" McQueen of Augusta, acclaimed for her role as Prissy in "Gone With the Wind" who also performs the role of "Queenie" in traveling productions of the musical, "Showboat," and had an opening role in "The Wiz" on Broadway which she quit after complaining about the smoking of marijuana in the audiences.

Blind Willie McTell, a blues and gospel singer who was born in Georgia and buried in McDuffie County after his death in 1959, was nominated posthumously for a Grammy in 1981 in the Best Ethnic or Traditional Recording category for his album, "Atlanta Blues: 1933."

Leroy Miller of Macon whose song "Hook Me, Then Reel Me in," got in Billboard's top 100 charts.

Paul Mitchell headed a jazz trio which entertained Atlantans at Dante's Down the Hatch for many years. Allen Murphy was the singer-percussionist and Layman Jackson the bassist.

Ruth Mitchell, a veteran of Broadway musicals, is credited with introducing jazz dance to Atlanta. She is from Decatur.

Jim Nabors, comedian and singer best known as television's Gomer Pyle, worked for Station WJBF-TV in Augusta before becoming a television and recording star.

Jimmy Nalls of Macon became famous with "Wet Willie" and Sea Level, a successful jazz-flavored group.

King Joe Oliver, famous blues singer who died in poverty in Savannah.

Bert Parks of Atlanta, national television personality, star of "The Music Man" and other Broadway musicals and for many years the singing master of ceremonies for the Miss America Pageant.

Uncle John Patterson, the self-proclaimed "Banjo King" from Carrollton once served in the Georgia General Assembly and picked with **Gordon Tanner,** Gid's son and **Smokey Joe Miller** from Walton County.

Minnie Pearl (Sara Ophelia Colley Cannon), Country Music Hall of Fame member and legendary performer on the Grand Ole Opry, once lived in Newnan.

Duke Pearson of Atlanta was one of the greatest jazzmen. He was an excellent composer, pianist, conductor and arranger. His original compositions number in the scores: "Cristo Redentor," "New Time Shuffle," "Chant" and "Sweet Honey Bee." He appeared at the Apollo Theater in New York and all over the world. He died in 1980 at the age of 48 from multiple sclerosis.

Margaret Perrin, Elbert County native and Atlanta institution, who has played piano at Noel Cowart's birthday party and entertained legions of Atlantans since she appeared in a kiddie review in the early days of WSB Radio.

Ivey Peterson was a country music comedian in Atlanta known to radio listeners as "Herman Horsehair Bugfuzz."

Pine Ridge Boys had the distinction of being the first to record the classic, "You Are My Sunshine." The two, Marvin Taylor and Doug Spivey, appeared on the Cross Roads Follies.

Joel Price, not only a talented comedian, the Lavonia native for many years played bass for Judy Lynn and Little Jimmy Dickens.

Georgia Prophets, a rock group founded in Augusta in the mid 1960's by the late Tommy Witcher, which recorded "Nobody Loves Me Like You" for Capricorn Records and featured the husband-and wife duo, Billy and Barbara Scott, as harmonizing vocalists.

Pylon the Athens Band which had a popular album, "Chomps," produced by Atlanta's independent DB Records.

Eddy Raven, the Louisiana singer, guitarist and songwriter who attended grade school in Savannah and high school in Metter and Baxley and made his first stage appearance in the winter of 1961 in the Cobbtown School Auditorium, is the author of hits "Country Green" and "Touch The Morning" for Don Gibson, "Good Morning Country Rain" for Jeannie C. Riley, "Back In The Country" for Roy Acuff, "Sometimes I Talk In My Sleep" for Randy Corner, "I Don't Want To Talk It Over Anymore" and "The Latest Shade of Blue" for Connie Smith. Raven has had recent hits for himself with "You're My Rainy Day Woman," "Thank God for Kids," and "I've Got Mexico."

Robert Ray who was New York's 1980 Entertainer of the Year moved to Atlanta thereafter where he and his group, The Rayettes, have become hits on the night and supper club circuits.

The Revelairs were a popular gospel group in the 50's. Bob Shaw, who became Georgia's Republican Chairman was a member.

Hoke and Paul Rice were a popular radio act in the Atlanta area during the 20's, 30's and 40's. Hoke was an influential guitarist that did session work for several record companies.

Bob and Babs Richardson who own and operate Mastersound Studios have been very active in NARAS and the Georgia Music Week festivities.

Ace Richman and the Sunshine Boys of Atlanta were a country and western singing group which performed on the WSB Radio Barn Dance and on the first television program of Station WEB-TV.

Ernest Rogers of Atlanta, columnist and amusements writer for The Atlanta Journal and an original performing personality on Radio Station WSB whose song, "Tune In My Heart," recorded by Ernie Hare was one of the first recordings played on radio.

Gamble Rogers, well liked and respected Lithia Springs resident, the "Daddy of Bluegrass Music in Georgia." Bluegrass Unlimited in a profile stated "his contribution to bluegrass has been equalled by few, if any, anywhere in the country."

Pam Rose, beautiful and diminutive singer from Atlanta, after

244

some success in Nashville as a solo artist now is part of the highly successful group **Calamity Jane.**

Art Rosenbaum is a nationally recognized scholar on folk music and has written an excellent book, "Folk Visions and Voices" about the traditional music of North Georgia. His wife and collaborator, Margo Newmark Rosenbaum, has photographed many folk singers in Georgia and throughout the world. Art, an artist and instructor at the University of Georgia, is a skilled banjo picker and has written an excellent book on that art.

Aunt Sarie (Sara Wilson) was part of an act on the Grand Ole Opry with her sister, Sallie, in the 1930's. The act broke up in the 1940's and "Aunt Sarie" came to Atlanta to entertain thousands.

Uncle Art Satherly, Country Music Hall of Fame member, Columbia Records producer and discoverer of Gene Autry, lived for many years in Savannah.

"Savannah," a group reminiscent of "Alabama," formed by two brothers from Albany, **Jay and Gene Willis** have had charted songs including "Back Street Ballet."

John Schneider of Atlanta, country singer and star of "The Dukes of Hazzard," got his start as a teen-aged star of The Crystal Pistol Revue at Six Flags Over Georgia.

Martha Scott, mezzo-soprano, Atlanta native and Clark College faculty member, is rated by many as one of the best soloist around.

Tommy Scott of Toccoa, operator of the last old-time medicine show on the road which tours some 350 towns throughout the United States and Canada each year. Scott got into the business during the Depression when he joined the show of "Doc" M. F. Chamberlain in Elberton. He has employed such western movie stars as Johnny Mack Brown, Kit Carson, Fuzzy St. John and Tim McCoy in his shows and had been inducted in the Country Music Association's Walkway of Stars. He has a showplace home in the North Georgia mountains which resembles a Chinese pagoda.

Sewanee Quintet of Augusta, the famous black gospel group which tours nationally and has recorded many gospel albums.

Shoal Creek Music Park has long been the home of the oldest bluegrass festival in Georgia. Owner **Alton Walters** brought Nashville stars to this park near Hartwell before any of the other parks were thought of.

Betty Smith appears at concerts throughout traditional Appalachian music and playing the dulcimer and other instruments.

Charlie Smithgall, Sr., of Gainesville, one of the first morning disc jockeys on America radio, was a star on Atlanta Radio Station WSB with the popular characters he created, "Daisy, the Calf" and "Professor Early Q. Wormcatcher," whose antics were interspersed with the playing of country music records.

Herman Spears of Atlanta, crooning singer on the original Barn Dance of Atlanta Radio Station WSB.

.38 Special had as one of its founders, Jeff Carlise of Atlanta, but most of this fine rock group grew up playing together in Jacksonville, Florida.

Roba Stanley: In 1924, she was country music's first "sweetheart," the forerunner of Loretta Lynn and other women of that caliber. She was the first female to sing solo on radio and on record. She is the daughter of R. M. Stanley, who was inducted into the Atlanta Country Music Hall of Fame in its second year; Roba was inducted during the first year. Her father was a champion fiddler. She now lives in Gainesville, Florida and remains physically active. She is in her late seventies and goes tubbing down the river frequently.

Starbuck, a premier rock group out of Atlanta, has had many hit records and their albums have sold well.

Carl Talton, "Cowboy Jack" as he was known, was an Atlanta radio performer for many years in the 30's, 40's and 50's.

Maude Thacker is a ballad singer from Tate who has a repertoire of British-American folk songs which she learned from her father in the 1920's.

Susan Thomas of Mountain Park sang back up for Tammy Wynette and wrote "The Woman in Me" which went to No. 3 in the charts for Crystal Gayle.

Willie Mae Thomas of Atlanta starred as "Little Nehi" on the WSB Barn Dance.

Bobby Thompson, bearded banjo player on Hee Haw, worked for Station WFBJ-TV in Augusta before becoming a much-in-demand session, backup and performing banjoist in Nashville.

The Upstairs, cabaret adjunct of Atlanta's famed Gene and Gabe's Restaurant which has been acclaimed for its original musical revues, the latest of which, "The Della Syndrome," was purchased for national presentation as a stage or television production.

Bob Van Camp of Atlanta, Music Director of Radio Station WSB succeeding Albert Coleman and virtuoso organist best known for his performances on "Mighty Mo," the Moler Organ in Atlanta's Fox Theater which is the world's largest theater organ.

Johnny Walker of Waycross has written a couple of hundred songs and has a dozen or more recorded by country music stars like Roy Acuff, Jack Greene and Ben Colter.

Agnes Ward of Columbus is a singer and dancer with Lena Horne.

Byron Warner of Atlanta was leader of the Seven Aces Orchestra which appeared regularly on Atlanta's Radio Station WSB before he moved to Athens to become Professor of Voice at the University of Georgia.

Belinda West of Augusta is a backup singer for Ronnie Milsap, a recording artist under contract to RCA and a singer of soul and gospel versions of commercials.

Libby Whittemore of Atlanta, pop singing star of musical revues at The Upstairs, the cabaret adjunct of Atlanta's famed Gene and Gabe's Restaurant.

Benji Wilhoite of Cartersville, talented young singer who has appeared in a number of films, including "Six Pack" with Kenny Rogers.

Larry Jon Wilson is a country singer and songwriter who was born on the Ohoopee River near Swainsboro and lived in North Augusta, South Carolina, before going to Nashville where he wrote and recorded his hit single, "Kindred Spirit," and the songs on his album, "Let Me Sing My Song For You" issued by Monument Records.

Eric Weisberg and **Steve Mandel,** the banjo duo who performed the classic "Dueling Banjos" for the soundtrack of the movie "Deliverance" which was filmed on Georgia's wild, scenic Chattooga River.

Mac Wiseman was appearing on the WSB Barn Dance when asked to join Bill Monroe.

Fletcher Wolfe is founder of the Atlanta Boys Choir. The group has performed concerts in Georgia for 25 years and annually tours Europe.

Randy Wood of Savannah was born in Douglas and is the designer and builder of custom guitars, mandolins and banjos. Users of his instruments and services include Jerry Redd, Michael "Wildfire" Murphy, J. J. Cale, Chet Atkins, Bill Monroe, Byron Berline, Roland White, Keith Richard and Eric Clapton.

Boots Woodall and the TV Wranglers, a country and western group, performed during the early days of television on Station WAGA-TV.

Ginny Wright, one of the only two female artists to record major hits with the late Jim Reeves during his lifetime was born in Twin City, Georgia, near Swainsboro, graduated from Emmanuel County Institute and now lives near the Midland Valley Golf Course between Augusta and Aiken, South Carolina. She and Reeves recorded "I Love You" which was No. 1 on the country charts for 23 weeks in 1953 and she did "Are You Mine" with Tom T. Hall which was No. 1 for 26 weeks. Others of her hits were the solo "I've Got Somebody New," "I Want You To Want Me" with Tom T. Hall and "I'm In Heaven" with Tom Bearden.

Steve Young who lived for some time in Newnan, Georgia, and played in Georgia honkytonks before moving to Nashville during the 1970's was called by Waylon Jennings "the second greatest country music singer — to George Jones, of course," who used his "Lonesome, Orn'ry and Mean" as the title track of one of his best albums. His own album, "Renegade Picker" done for RCA in 1976 was praised by critics, but so far a major hit has eluded him.

And there are many, many more that I don't know about . . . talented artists I would admire and put in this book if our paths had crossed. Keep on pickin' and singing and I hope to hear you soon.

ZELL MILLER